HARCOURT
Science

Harcourt School Publishers

Orlando • Boston • Dallas • Chicago • San Diego

www.harcourtschool.com

Cover Image
This frog is a reticulated clown tree frog. It is found in the rainforest surrounding the Amazon river valley in Peru.

Printed in the United States of America

ISBN 0-15-315698-8 UNIT A
ISBN 0-15-315699-6 UNIT B
ISBN 0-15-315700-3 UNIT C
ISBN 0-15-315701-1 UNIT D
ISBN 0-15-315702-X UNIT E
ISBN 0-15-315703-8 UNIT F

11 12 13 14 15 032 10 09 08 07 06 05 04 03

Authors

Marjorie Slavick Frank
Former Adjunct Faculty Member at Hunter, Brooklyn, and Manhattan Colleges
New York, New York

Robert M. Jones
Professor of Education
University of Houston-Clear Lake
Houston, Texas

Gerald H. Krockover
Professor of Earth and Atmospheric Science Education
School Mathematics and Science Center
Purdue University
West Lafayette, Indiana

Mozell P. Lang
Science Education Consultant
Michigan Department of Education
Lansing, Michigan

Joyce C. McLeod
Visiting Professor
Rollins College
Winter Park, Florida

Carol J. Valenta
Vice President—Education, Exhibits, and Programs
St. Louis Science Center
St. Louis, Missouri

Barry A. Van Deman
Science Program Director
Arlington, Virginia

Senior Editorial Advisor

Napoleon Adebola Bryant, Jr.
Professor Emeritus of Education
Xavier University
Cincinnati, Ohio

Program Advisors

Michael J. Bell
Assistant Professor of Early Childhood Education
School of Education
University of Houston-Clear Lake
Houston, Texas

George W. Bright
Professor of Mathematics Education
The University of North Carolina at Greensboro
Greensboro, North Carolina

Pansy Cowder
Science Specialist
Tampa, Florida

Nancy Dobbs
Science Specialist, Heflin Elementary
Alief ISD
Houston, Texas

Robert H. Fronk
Head, Science/Mathematics Education Department
Florida Institute of Technology
Melbourne, Florida

Gloria R. Guerrero
Education Consultant
Specialist in English as a Second Language
San Antonio, Texas

Bernard A. Harris, Jr.
Physician and Former Astronaut
(STS 55—Space Shuttle Columbia, STS 63—Space Shuttle Discovery)
Vice President, SPACEHAB Inc.
Houston, Texas

Lois Harrison-Jones
Education and Management Consultant
Dallas, Texas

Linda Levine
Educational Consultant
Orlando, Florida

Bertie Lopez
Curriculum and Support Specialist
Ysleta ISD
El Paso, Texas

Kenneth R. Mechling
Professor of Biology and Science Education
Clarion University of Pennsylvania
Clarion, Pennsylvania

Nancy Roser
Professor of Language and Literacy Studies
University of Texas, Austin
Austin, Texas

Program Advisor and Activities Writer

Barbara ten Brink
Science Director
Round Rock Independent School District
Round Rock, Texas

Reviewers and Contributors

Jay Bell
K-6 Science Specialist, Curriculum Department
Lodi Unified School District
Lodi, California

Roland Boucher
Principal, Fox and Burnham Schools
Haverhill, Massachussetts

Dorothy J. Finnell
Curriculum Consultant
Houston, Texas

Kathy Jo Graley
Teacher, Kenna Elementary
Charleston, West Virginia

Gary D. Gray
Teacher, Eastern Hills Elementary
Fort Worth ISD
Fort Worth, Texas

Teresa McMillan
Teacher-in-Residence
University of Houston-Clear Lake
Houston, Texas

Clyde Partner
Science/Health Curriculum Coordinator
Evanston S.D. #65
Evanston, Illinois

Michael F. Ryan
Educational Technology Specialist
Lake County Schools
Tavares, Florida

Judy Taylor
Teacher, Silvestri Junior High School
Las Vegas, Nevada

UNIT A

LIFE SCIENCE

Processes of Living Things

UNIT B

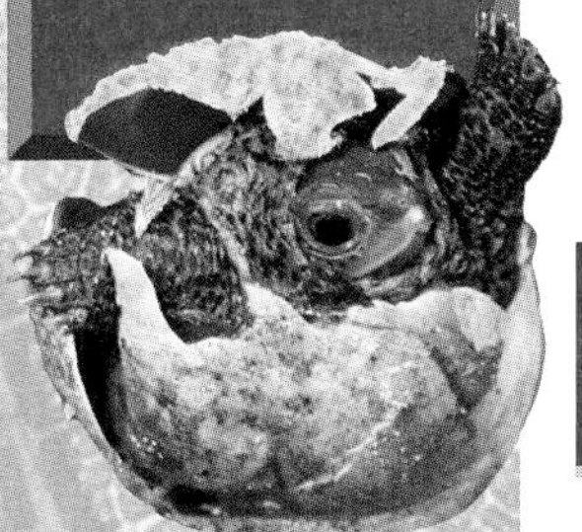

LIFE SCIENCE

Systems and Interactions in Nature

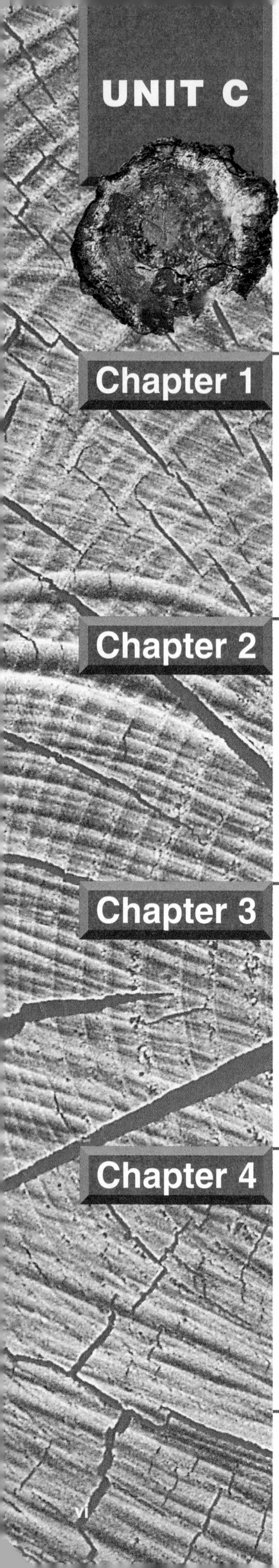

UNIT C

EARTH SCIENCE

Processes That Change The Earth

UNIT D

EARTH SCIENCE

The Solar System and Beyond

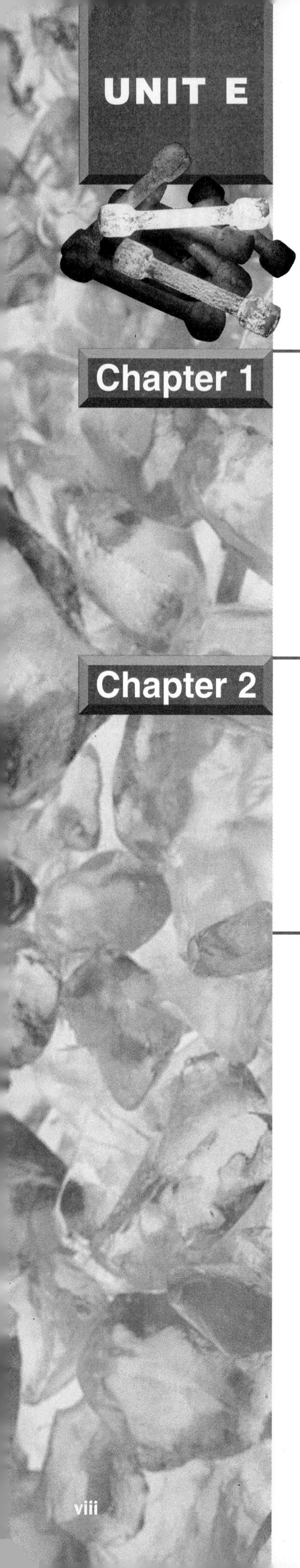

UNIT E

PHYSICAL SCIENCE

Building Blocks of Matter

Chapter 1

Matter and Its Properties E2

Chapter 2

Atoms and Elements E34

UNIT F

PHYSICAL SCIENCE

Energy and Motion

Using Science Process Skills

When scientists try to find an answer to a question or do an experiment, they use thinking tools called process skills. You use many of the process skills whenever you think, listen, read, and write. Think about how these students used process skills to help them answer questions and do experiments.

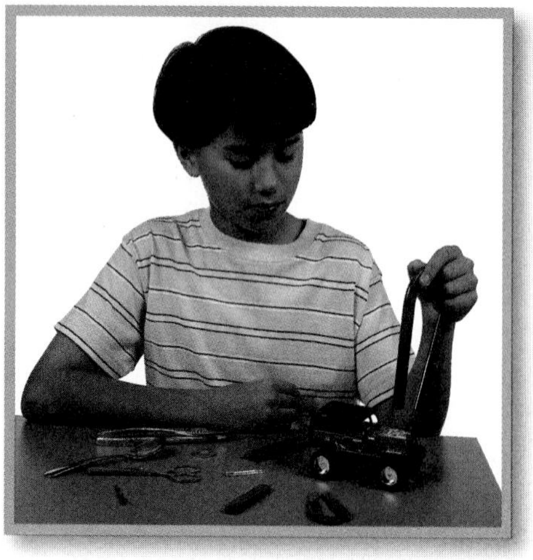

Greg is finding leaves for his leaf collection. He carefully **observes** the leaves and **compares** their shapes, sizes, and colors. He **measures** each leaf with a ruler. Then he **classifies** the leaves into groups by their sizes.

Try This Use the process skills of observing, comparing, measuring, and classifying to organize your own collection of nature objects.

Talk About It By what other characteristics could Greg classify the leaves in his collection?

Process Skills

Observe—use the senses to learn about objects and events

Compare—identify characteristics of things or events to find out how they are alike and different

Measure—compare an attribute of an object, such as its mass, length, or volume, to a standard unit such as a gram, a centimeter, or liter

Classify—group or organize objects or events in categories based on specific characteristics

It is a rainy Monday. Pilar wants to know if it will rain during the coming weekend. She **gathers** and **records** data to make a prediction about the weather. She observes the weather each day of the week and records it. She **displays** the data on a chart. On Friday, she **predicts**, based on her observations, that it will rain during the weekend.

Try This Beginning on a Monday, gather data about the temperature at noon. Record your data. Repeat this for four more days. Find a way to display your data. Then predict what the temperature will be at noon on Saturday.

Talk About It Why do you think Pilar predicted it would rain during the weekend?

Process Skills

Gather Data — make observations and use them to make inferences or predictions

Record Data — write down observations

Display Data — make tables, charts, or graphs

Predict — form an idea of an expected outcome based on observations or experience

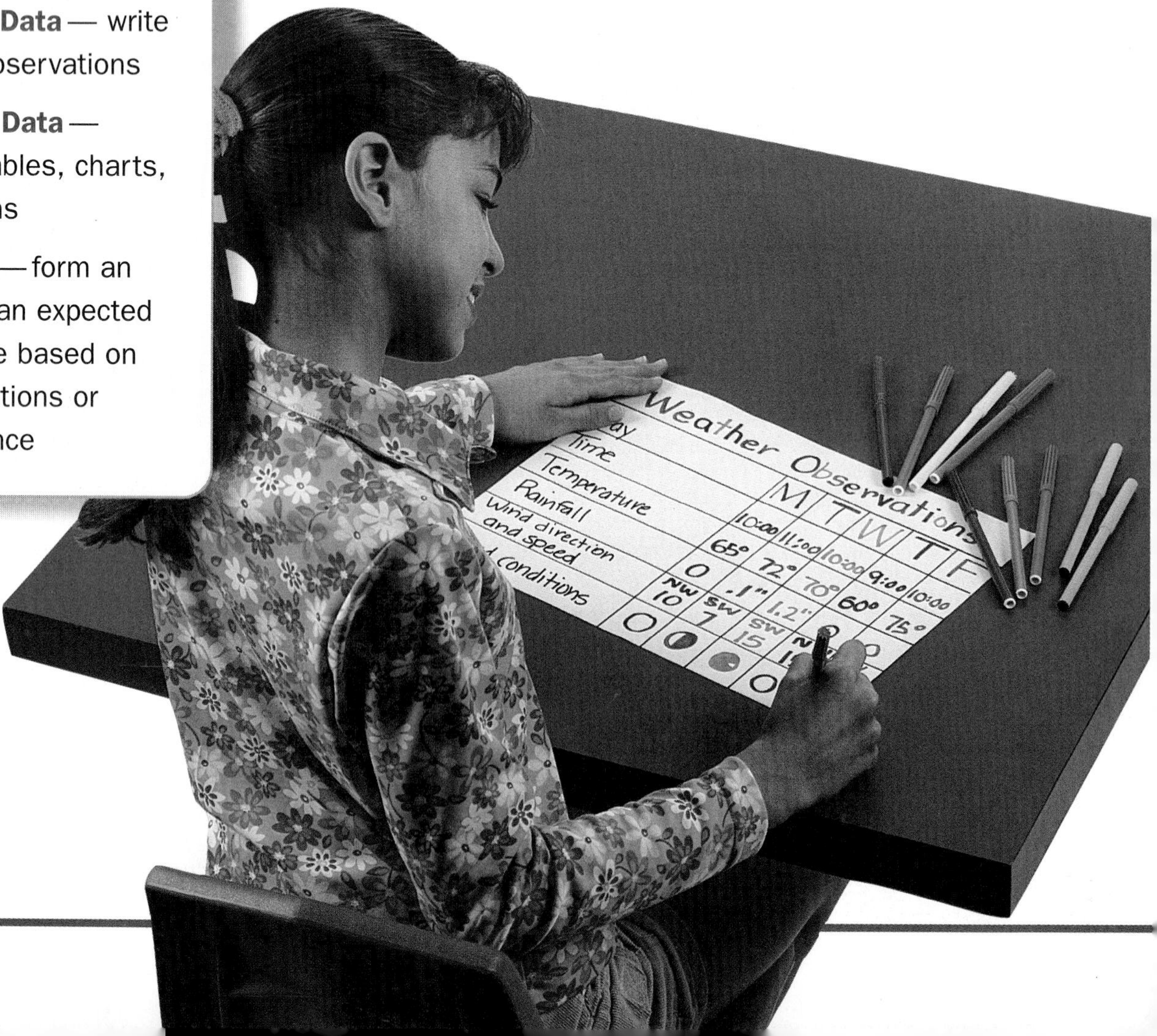

Kim is interested in knowing how the size of a magnet is related to its strength. He **hypothesizes** that larger magnets are stronger than smaller magnets. He **plans and conducts a simple investigation** to see if his hypothesis is correct. He gathers magnets of different sizes. He finds items of different weights that the magnet will attract. He tests each item on each magnet, and records his findings. His hypothesis is correct until he tests the last item, a toy truck. When the largest horseshoe magnet cannot pick up the truck, but a smaller bar magnet can, he **infers** that the largest magnet is usually the strongest, but not always.

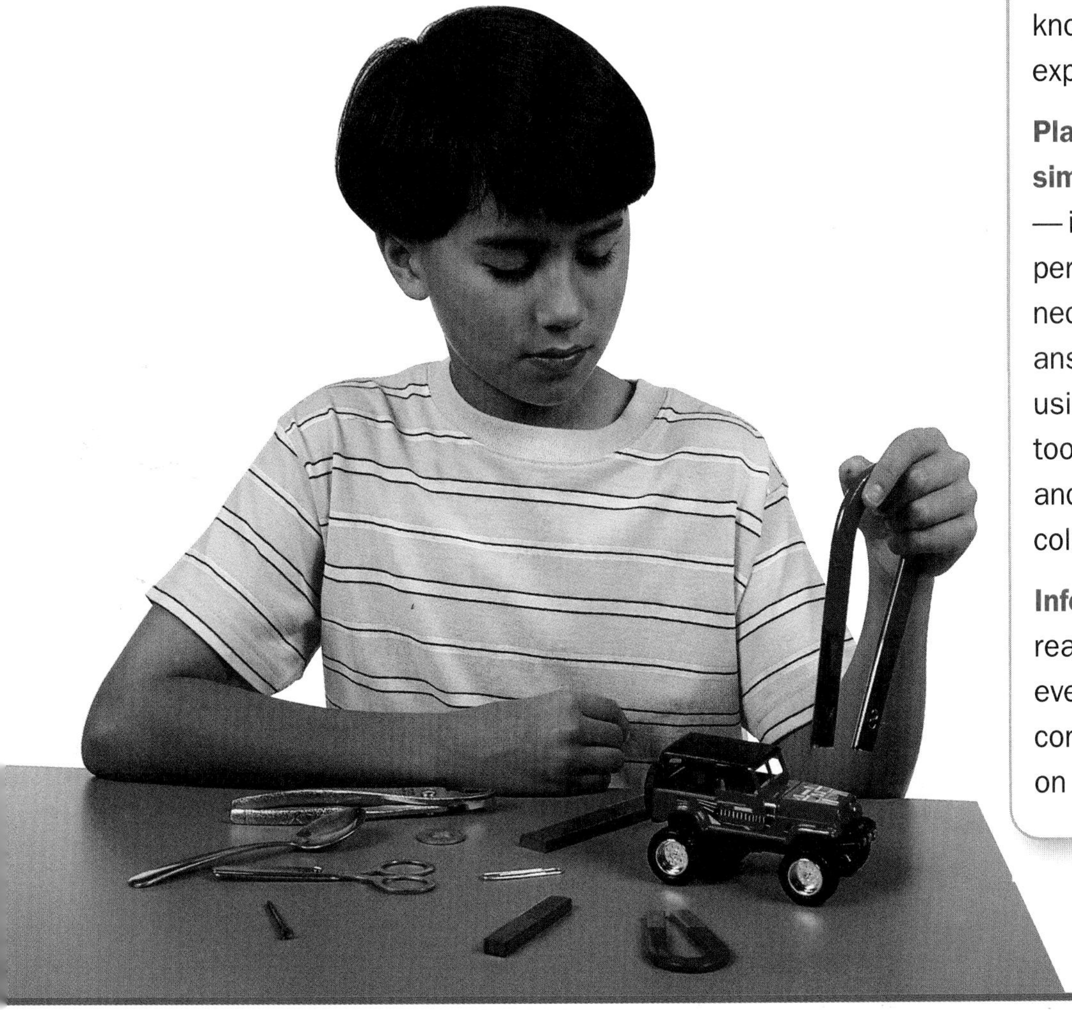

Try This Make a hypothesis about something you are interested in. Plan and conduct an investigation to test your hypothesis.

Talk About It Kim used different shapes of magnets as well as different sizes in his investigation. Do you think this could make a difference in the results? Why or why not?

Process Skills

Hypothesize — make a statement about the expected outcome based on observation, knowledge, and experience

Plan and conduct simple investigations — identify and perform the steps necessary to find the answer to a question, using appropriate tools and recording and analyzing the data collected

Infer — use logical reasoning to explain events and draw conclusions based on observations

Emily sees an ad about food wrap. The people in the ad claim that Tight-Right food wrap seals containers better than other food wraps. She plans a simple investigation to find out if this claim is true.

Emily **identifies and controls the variables** by choosing three bowls that are exactly the same. She labels the bowls A, B, and C. She places the bowls on a tray, and puts exactly 250 mL of water in each bowl. She cuts a 25-cm piece of Tight-Right wrap and places it on top of bowl A. She places 25-cm pieces of other brands of wrap on bowls B and C. She seals the wrap to the top of all three bowls as tightly as she can.

Emily **experiments** with the seals by pulling sharply on the tray. The water sloshes up the sides of the bowls. Water does not leak out the top of bowl A. On bowls B and C, the seals are broken, and water has spilled over onto the tray. From her observations, Emily infers that the claim for Tight-Right wrap is true.

Try This Plan an experiment to test different brands of a product your family uses. Identify the variables that you will control.

Talk About It Why did Emily use the tray in her experiment?

Process Skills

Identify and Control Variables — identify and control factors that affect the outcome of an experiment

Experiment — design ways to collect data to test hypotheses under controlled conditions

You will have many opportunities to practice and apply these and other process skills in *Harcourt Science*. An exciting year of science discoveries lies ahead!

Safety in Science

Doing investigations in science can be fun, but you need to be sure you do them safely. Here are some rules to follow.

1. **Think ahead.** Study the steps of the investigation so you know what to expect. If you have any questions, ask your teacher. Be sure you understand any safety symbols that are shown.
2. **Be neat.** Keep your work area clean. If you have long hair, pull it back so it doesn't get in the way. Roll or push up long sleeves to keep them away from your experiment.
3. **Oops!** If you should spill or break something, or get cut, tell your teacher right away.
4. **Watch your eyes.** Wear safety goggles anytime you are directed to do so. If you get anything in your eyes, tell your teacher right away.
5. **Yuck!** Never eat or drink anything during a science activity.
6. **Don't get shocked.** Be especially careful if an electric appliance is used. Be sure that electric cords are in a safe place where you can't trip over them. Don't ever pull a plug out of an outlet by pulling on the cord.
7. **Keep it clean.** Always clean up when you have finished. Put everything away and wipe your work area. Wash your hands.

In some activities you will see these symbols. They are signs for what you need to be safe.

Be especially careful.

Wear safety goggles.

Be careful with sharp objects.

Don't get burned.

Protect your clothes.

Protect your hands with mitts.

Be careful with electricity.

UNIT C

EARTH SCIENCE

Processes that Change the Earth

Unit Project

Earth Surface Scrapbook

Cut from magazines and newspapers pictures of processes that change the surface of Earth. Organize your pictures into a scrapbook. Identify the process that is or was taking place in each picture, and describe how the surface of Earth was changed.

Chapter 1

Vocabulary Preview

landform
weathering
erosion
deposition
mass movement
crust
mantle
core
plate
magma
volcano
earthquake
fault
continental drift
Pangea
fossil

Changes to Earth's Surface

The expression "on solid ground" means that you are certain about something. But there is really no such thing as solid ground—the ground we stand on is always moving.

FAST FACT

In May 1980 Mount St. Helens, a volcano in Washington State, erupted. Ash from the eruption covered an area of more than 22,000 square miles.

FAST FACT

There are more than half a million earthquakes every year. Most occur at the bottom of the ocean and are too small to be felt. Only about 1000 earthquakes a year cause any damage.

FAST FACT

Mauna Kea, a dormant volcano on the island of Hawai'i, is one of the tallest mountains in the world. From the floor of the Pacific Ocean it rises 9750 m (about 32,000 ft) to sea level and 4205 m (13,796 ft) above sea level, for a total height of nearly 14,000 m (about 46,000 ft). By comparison, Mount Everest is 8848 m (about 29,000 ft) high.

LESSON 1

What Processes Change Landforms?

In this lesson, you can . . .

INVESTIGATE how water cuts through sand.

LEARN ABOUT how wind, water, and ice shape landforms.

LINK to math, writing, social studies, and technology.

▼ Sand carried by wind can carve desert rock into unusual shapes.

INVESTIGATE

How Water Changes Earth's Surface

Activity Purpose Moving water is the most powerful force there is for changing Earth's surface. It can move soil, make cliffs fall down, and carve canyons in solid rock. In this investigation, you will **use a model**—a stream table—to **observe** how moving water can cut through sand.

Materials

- stream table
- sand
- 2 lengths of plastic tubing
- 2 plastic pails
- 3 wood blocks
- water

Activity Procedure

1. Place the stream table on a classroom table. Make sure the front end of the stream table is even with the edge of the table. Put the stream-table support under the back end of the stream table. (Picture A)
2. Fill the stream table with sand.
3. Using two fingers, make a path, or channel, down the middle of the sand.
4. Connect one end of one length of tubing to the front of the stream table. Let the other end of the tubing hang over the edge of the table. Place an empty pail on the floor under the hanging end of the tubing. (Picture B)

Picture A

Picture B

5. Place the other pail on two wood blocks near the raised end of the stream-table channel. Fill this pail $\frac{3}{4}$ full of water.
6. Put the second length of tubing into the pail, and fill it with water.
7. Start the water flowing through the tube from the pail to the stream table by lowering one end of the filled tube.
8. **Observe** any changes the water makes to the sand in the stream table. **Record** your observations.
9. Place the third wood block on top of the support under the stream table. Repeat Steps 7 and 8.

Draw Conclusions

1. In which setup was the speed of the water greater?
2. In which setup did you **observe** greater movement of sand from the channel?
3. **Scientists at Work** Scientists learn by **observing.** What did you learn about the way water can change the land by observing the channel in the stream table?

Investigate Further **Hypothesize** what would happen if you replaced the sand with soil. **Experiment** to test your hypothesis.

Process Skill Tip

When you use your eyes to notice how the sand looks before and after water flows through it, you **observe** a change. Careful observations are important in science.

LEARN ABOUT

Changes to Earth's Surface

FIND OUT

- how Earth's crust is broken down into soil
- how water, wind, and ice change landforms

VOCABULARY

landforms
weathering
erosion
deposition
mass movement

Changing Landforms

Earth's surface is changing all around you. Rivers wear away rock and produce deep canyons. Waves eat away at sea cliffs, turning them into beach sand. Glaciers scrape away the tops of mountains, and winds carrying sand grind away desert rock. Earth's **landforms**, physical features on its surface, might seem as if they never change, but they do.

In the investigation, you saw how the force of flowing water can move sand. Forces such as flowing water, waves, wind, ice, and even movements inside the Earth are constantly changing landforms. Sometimes the changes happen fast enough for you to observe. For example, a volcano might erupt suddenly and blow away a mountaintop, or a powerful hurricane might sweep away a sandy beach. But most changes to Earth's landforms happen so slowly that you cannot observe them directly. Sometimes you can see only the results of past changes.

✓ What are some of the forces that change landforms?

◄ Thousands of years of rain and wind shaped these landforms in Utah's Monument Valley.

Flowing water cuts into riverbanks and carries away soil. ▼

◄ The pounding of ocean waves slowly wears away rocky cliffs.

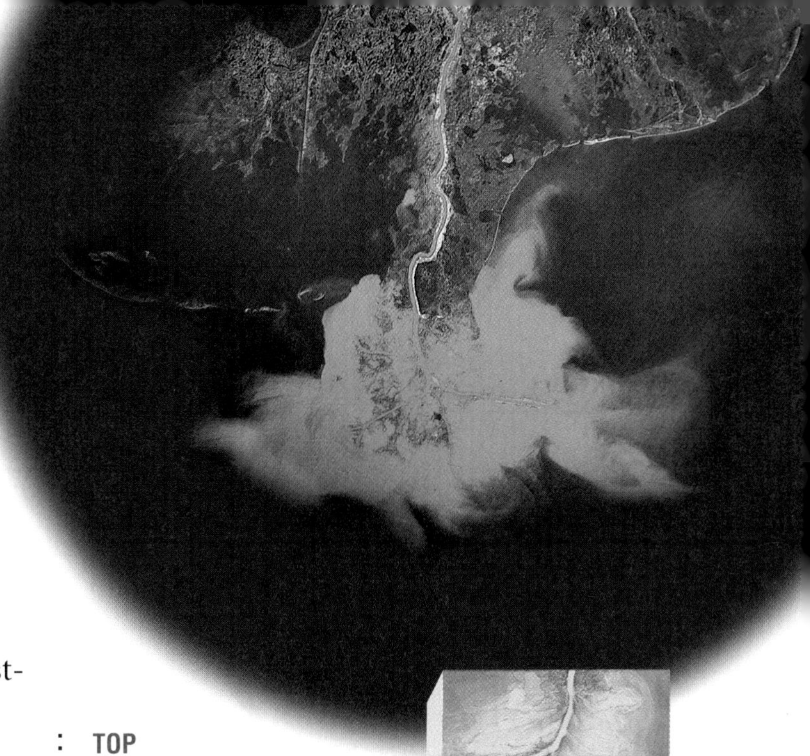

This satellite photo shows the delta the Mississippi River has built in the Gulf of Mexico. ►

Water

Much of Earth's surface is made of rock. The shaping of landforms starts when weathering wears away rock. **Weathering** is the process of breaking rock into soil, sand, and other tiny pieces, or particles, called *sediment.* Water is an important agent, or cause, of weathering.

Water weathers rock in several ways. Fast-flowing rivers can carve deep canyons in rock. Arizona's Grand Canyon, carved by the action of the Colorado River, is 1.6 km (about 1 mi) deep. Also, ocean waves can weather cliffs and cause them to fall into the sea. Water can weather rock in other ways, too. When it rains, water seeps into tiny holes, or pores, and cracks in rock. If this water freezes, it expands, breaking the rock. Rain that becomes acidic because of pollution can dissolve rock. And flowing water tumbles rocks against each other, breaking them into smaller pieces and smoothing their edges.

After weathering has broken rock into sediment, erosion and deposition move the sediment around and leave it in new places. **Erosion** (ee•ROH•zhuhn) is the process of moving sediment from one place to another. **Deposition** (dep•uh•ZISH•uhn) is the process of dropping, or depositing, sediment in a new location.

Water is not only an important agent of weathering but also the chief agent of erosion. Water can erode great amounts of sediment. At the shore, sediment from weathered cliffs is eroded by waves and deposited as new sand on beaches. Rainfall erodes sediment and carries it into rivers and streams. Rivers pick up the sediment and move it downstream. Most rivers deposit sediment in flat areas along their banks. These *flood plains,* as they are called, can become rich agricultural areas. Some rivers deposit sediment in broad areas at their mouths. These areas of new land are called *deltas.* The Mississippi River delta is one of the largest in the world.

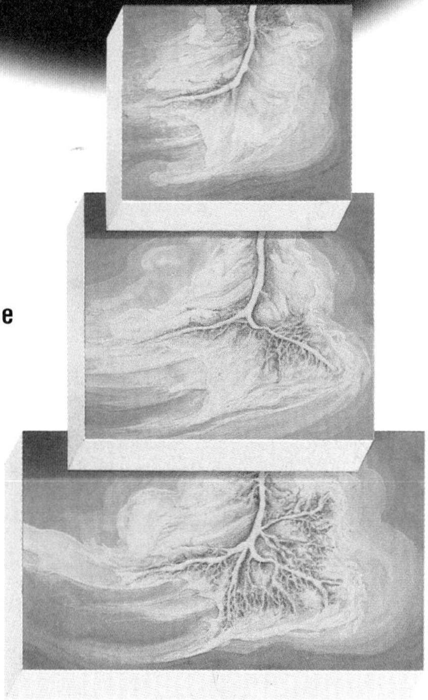

TOP
Deltas form as rivers slow down and deposit sediment at their mouths.

CENTER
As the delta builds, the river separates into smaller channels.

BOTTOM
The number of channels continues to increase. Each one becomes a place where sediment is deposited.

✔ **What is the difference between weathering and erosion?**

Wind

Wind is another agent of weathering and erosion. Have you ever seen a machine called a sandblaster? It uses a powerful jet of air containing sand to clean building surfaces. In a similar way, wind can carry bits of rock and sand that weather rock surfaces. Wind also moves sediment from place to place. If the wind blows hard, it can erode a lot of sediment.

In dry areas like the American Southwest, wind erosion has shaped some of the world's most unusual landforms—rocks that look like tables, arches, or columns. Wind erodes dry sediment more easily than it erodes particles of soil or damp rock. And there is little plant life in dry areas to hold sediment in place.

Wind erosion can also blow sand into large mounds called *dunes*. Huge dunes as much as 100 m (about 325 ft) high form in some deserts. Many sandy beaches have long lines of dunes on their land side. Beach dunes are built by the constantly blowing sea breezes. They help protect the land behind them during storms.

✓ How does wind erosion change landforms?

Ice

Ice in the form of glaciers can also change landforms. *Glaciers* are thick sheets of ice, formed in areas where more snow falls during the winter than melts during the summer. Glaciers seem to stand still, but they actually move. Because of a glacier's great size and weight, it erodes everything under it. Glaciers erode sediment from one place and deposit it in another.

There are two kinds of glaciers. *Valley glaciers* are found in high mountain valleys. They flow slowly down mountainsides, eroding the mountain under them and forming U-shaped valleys. Only a few valley glaciers remain in North America. And even those are melting rapidly.

Continental glaciers are ice sheets that cover large areas of Earth. They cover almost all of Greenland and Antarctica today. But thousands of years ago, when the climate was colder, continental glaciers covered Europe, Canada, and the northern United States.

✓ What are glaciers?

Dunes form where an obstacle, such as a plant or a rock, causes wind to slow and deposit the sand it is carrying. ▼

The Athabasca Glacier recedes about 13 m (43 ft) each year. During the past 100 years, it has receded about 1.6 km (1 mi). ►

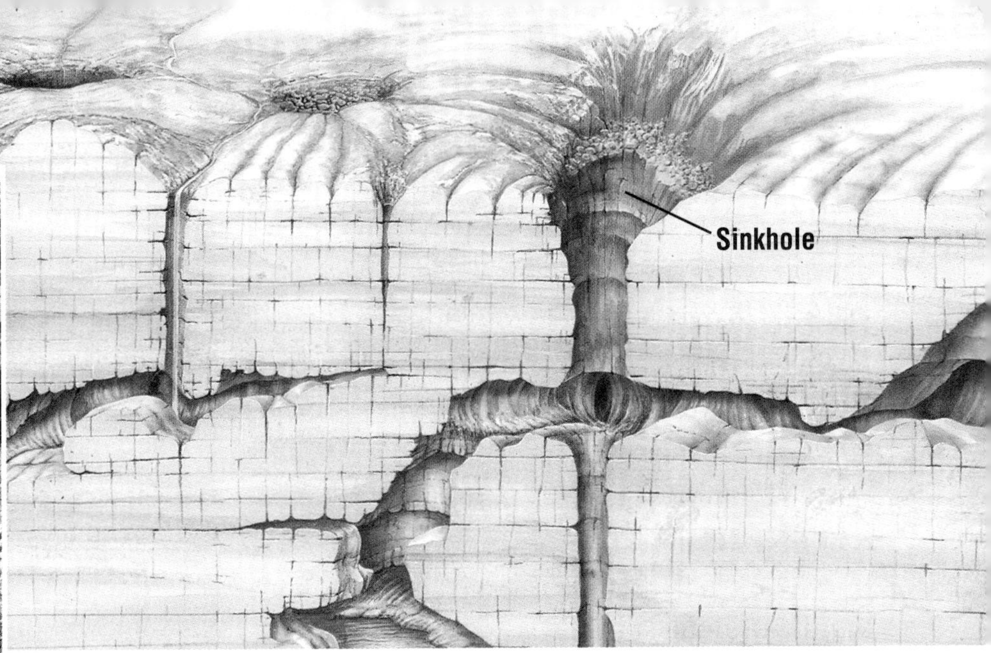

◀ The Winter Park sinkhole was large enough to swallow cars and buildings.

▲ Acid rainwater easily dissolves soft rock, such as limestone.

Mass Movement

During the winter of 1997–1998, heavy rains fell on much of the California coast. One night, families living in a small canyon heard a loud noise. When they went outside to see what had happened, they discovered that a mound of mud had slid down the steep sides of the canyon, covering part of a house. This mudslide occurred when a mass of soil that was full of water moved rapidly downhill.

A mudslide is one type of mass movement. **Mass movement** is the downhill movement of rock and soil because of gravity. Mass movements, such as mudslides and landslides, can change landforms quickly. Mudslides move wet soil. Landslides move dry soil. Landslides occur when gravity becomes stronger than the friction that holds soil in place on a hill. The soil falls suddenly to the bottom of the hill.

Another type of mass movement—one that occurs slowly, as you might guess from its name—is called *creep*. Creep occurs when soil moves slowly downhill because of gravity. Creep is so slow that changes in landforms are hard to observe directly. The land may move only a few centimeters each year. But over time, creep can move fences, utility poles, roads, and railroad tracks.

One day in 1981, in the city of Winter Park, Florida, an area of land suddenly collapsed, or fell in on itself. The hole swallowed houses, swimming pools, and businesses, including a car dealership. Today there is a lake where there was once dry land. The process that led to the formation of the Winter Park sinkhole is different from that of other types of mass movement.

A sinkhole is a large hole in the ground that opens suddenly. Sinkholes form after rock under the surface has dissolved or become weak. Sinkholes often appear in areas of limestone rock, because limestone dissolves easily. Rain seeping into the ground combines with carbon dioxide from the air to form a weak acid called *carbonic acid*. Carbonic acid dissolves limestone, forming huge holes. When enough rock has dissolved, land over the weakened area collapses.

✔ **What is mass movement?**

New Landforms

Erosion and deposition can change landforms or produce new ones. Rivers can deposit sediment that builds deltas. They can also change their path, or course, producing new lakes on wide flood plains.

Glaciers are major forces for forming new landforms. As the glaciers of the last Ice Age moved forward, they pushed mounds of rock and soil in front of them. When the glaciers melted, they left behind at their lower ends long ridges of soil and rock, called *terminal moraines.* Long Island and Cape Cod are terminal moraines. They mark the leading edge of the glacier that covered much of North America.

New islands can be formed by volcanic eruptions. Underwater volcanoes increase their height by depositing melted rock and ash. In time, they break through the sea surface as islands. The Hawaiian Islands formed in this way. Almost constant eruptions of Kilauea add daily to the size of the island of Hawai'i. Another volcano, now growing slowly on the ocean floor east of Hawai'i, will one day become the island of Hohonu.

✓ What new landforms are created by erosion and deposition?

Old, slow-moving rivers form broad loops. ▼

The loops can become so broad that they meet. ▼

Because the river follows the shortest route, its flow cuts off the loop. The old loop forms a crescent-shaped body of water called an *oxbow lake.* ▼

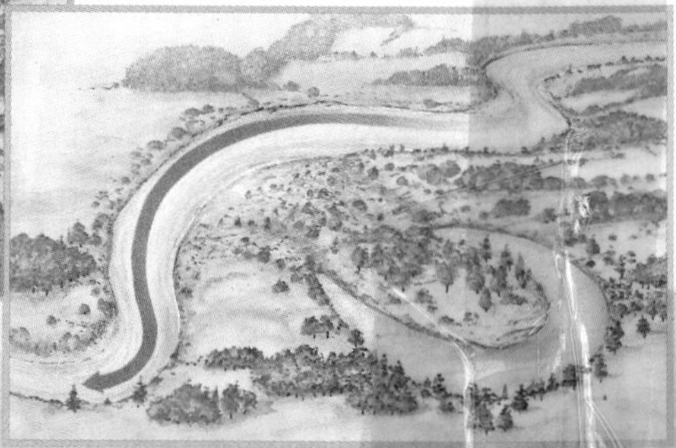

Mississippi River, south of Memphis, Tennessee ▼

Summary

Weathering breaks down the rock of Earth's surface into soil, sand, and other small particles. Agents of erosion, such as water, wind, and ice, change Earth's landforms by moving rock and soil. Water can carve canyons and deposit sediment to form deltas. Wind can form sand dunes. Ice can carve U-shaped valleys and leave landforms such as terminal moraines. Even forces within the Earth, such as volcanoes, can produce new landforms.

Review

1. What is erosion?
2. What is deposition?
3. What forces cause erosion and deposition?
4. **Critical Thinking** Why is weathering so important to life on land?
5. **Test Prep** A type of mass movement is a —
   A glacier
   B delta
   C mudslide
   D terminal moraine

LINKS

MATH LINK

Glacier Size The Aletsch Glacier in Europe is 80 km^2. Malaspina Glacier in Alaska measures 1344 km^2. The Grinnell Glacier in Montana is about 2 km^2. Use a computer, if possible, to make a bar graph that compares these glaciers.

WRITING LINK

Informative Writing—Description During the 1930s huge dust storms eroded large areas of the Great Plains of the United States. Find out what caused the Dust Bowl, as the eroded region was called, and what problems it led to. Write a story for your teacher describing the Dust Bowl from the point of view of someone who lived there.

SOCIAL STUDIES LINK

Topographic Maps Topographic maps use symbols and colors to represent landforms. These maps can tell you how the land looks—if you know how to read them. At the library, look for a topographic map of the area where you live. What kinds of symbols are used to show water, wetlands, and deserts?

TECHNOLOGY LINK

Learn more about landscapes and erosion by visiting this Internet site.
www.scilinks.org/harcourt

SCILINKS™ THE WORLD'S A CLICK AWAY

LESSON 2

What Causes Mountains, Volcanoes, and Earthquakes?

In this lesson, you can . . .

INVESTIGATE the structure of Earth.

LEARN ABOUT what forms mountains and volcanoes.

LINK to math, writing, literature, and technology.

Volcanoes release melted rock from deep inside Earth. ▼

INVESTIGATE

Journey to the Center of Earth

Activity Purpose If you could slice Earth in half, you would see that it has several layers. Of course, you can't slice Earth in half, but you can make a model of it. In this investigation you will **make a model** that shows Earth's layers.

Materials

- 2 graham crackers
- 1 small plastic bag
- disposable plastic gloves
- 1 spoon
- 1 jar peanut butter
- 1 hazelnut or other round nut
- freezer
- plastic knife

Activity Procedure

1. Put the graham crackers in the plastic bag. Close the bag and use your hands to crush the crackers into crumbs. Then set the bag aside.
2. Put on the plastic gloves. Use the spoon to scoop a glob of peanut butter from the jar and put it in your gloved hand. Place the nut in the center of the peanut butter. Cover the nut with more peanut butter until there is about 2.5 cm of peanut butter all around the nut. Using both hands, roll the glob of peanut butter with the nut at its center into a ball. (Picture A)

Picture A

Picture B

3. Open the bag of crushed graham crackers, and roll the peanut butter ball in the graham cracker crumbs until the outside of the ball is completely coated.

4. Put the ball in the freezer for about 15 minutes. Remove the ball and cut into your model with the plastic knife. **Observe** the layers inside. You might want to take a photograph of your model for later review. (Picture B)

Draw Conclusions

1. The peanut butter ball is a model of Earth's layers. How many layers does Earth have in this model?
2. Which layer of Earth do the crushed graham crackers represent? Why do you think your model has a thick layer of peanut butter but a thin layer of graham cracker crumbs?
3. **Scientists at Work** Scientists can see and understand complex structures better by **making models** of them. What does the model show about Earth's layers? What doesn't the model show about Earth's layers?

Investigate Further Some geologists, scientists who study the Earth, say that Earth's center is divided into a soft outer part and a hard inner part. How could you **make a model** to show this?

Process Skill Tip

You cannot see Earth's layers. So **making a model** helps you understand how they look in relation to each other. In this activity, you need to cut open the model to see the layers.

Mountains, Volcanoes, and Earthquakes

FIND OUT

- how mountains form
- what causes volcanoes and earthquakes

VOCABULARY

crust
mantle
core
plate
magma
volcano
earthquake
fault

Earth's Interior

As the model you made in the investigation showed, Earth is not a solid ball of rock. It has three distinct layers. We live on Earth's crust. The **crust** is the outer layer, and it is made of rock. Earth's crust is very thin compared to the other layers. If Earth were the size of a chicken's egg, the crust would be thinner than the egg's shell.

The **mantle** is the layer of rock beneath Earth's crust. Just under the crust, the rock of the mantle is solid. But the mantle is very hot. This makes part of the mantle soft, like melted candy. No one has ever been to the mantle, but soft, hot rock from the mantle sometimes reaches Earth's surface through volcanoes.

The **core** is the center layer of Earth. It is Earth's hottest layer. The core can be divided into two parts: an outer core of liquid, or *molten,* iron and an inner core of solid iron. Even though the core is very hot, great pressure at the center of Earth keeps the inner core solid.

✔ **What parts of Earth are solid rock?**

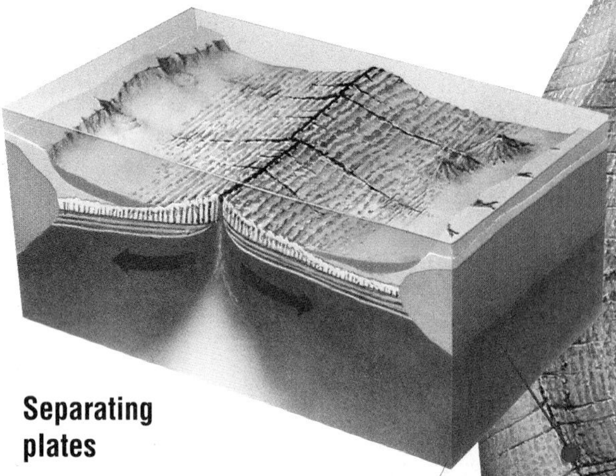

Separating plates

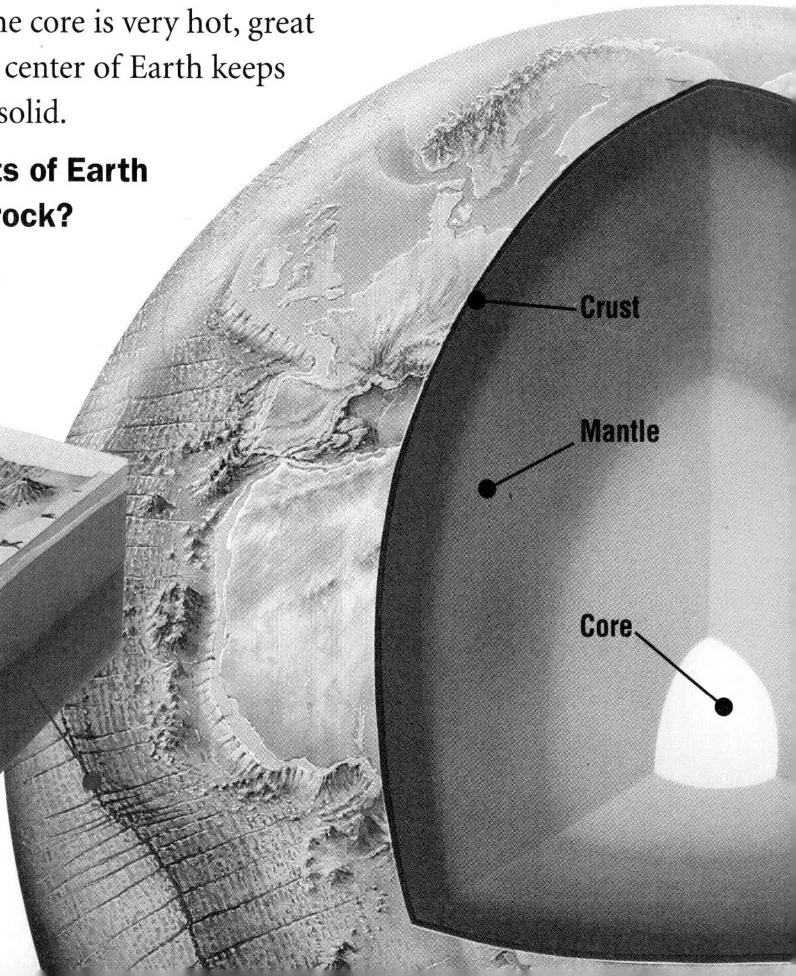

Earth's Crust Moves

Earth's surface is not a single piece of rock. Instead, it is made up of many plates. **Plates** are rigid blocks of crust and upper mantle rock. Most of North America, Greenland, and the western half of the North Atlantic Ocean are on the North American plate. Part of California and most of the Pacific Ocean make up the Pacific plate. There are 12 major plates in all. Earth's plates fit together like the pieces of a jigsaw puzzle.

Although these plates are enormous, they actually float on the soft rock of the mantle. Pressure and heat within the Earth produce currents in the soft rock of the mantle. As the mantle moves, the plates floating on it move, too.

Plate movement is very slow—only a few centimeters each year. But because plates are right next to each other, the movement of one plate affects other plates. Some plates push together. Some pull apart. Other plates slide past each other. As plates move around, they cause great changes in Earth's landforms.

Where plates collide, energy is released, and new landforms are produced. On land, mountains rise and volcanoes erupt. South America's Andes Mountains are a result of the Nazca and South American plates colliding. On the ocean floor, deep trenches form.

As plates pull apart on land, valleys dotted with volcanoes develop. Africa's Great Rift Valley was formed by the African and Arabian plates pulling apart. The rift, or crack, will one day result in a complete separation of part of eastern Africa from the rest of the continent. Where plates pull apart under the sea, ridges and volcanoes form. This spreading forms new sea floor at the ridges.

When plates scrape and slide past each other, they shake Earth's surface. Along the San Andreas (an•DRAY•uhs) fault in California, the Pacific plate is moving past the North American plate. The plates rub and shake as they grind past each other, causing earthquakes.

✓ **What are Earth's plates?**

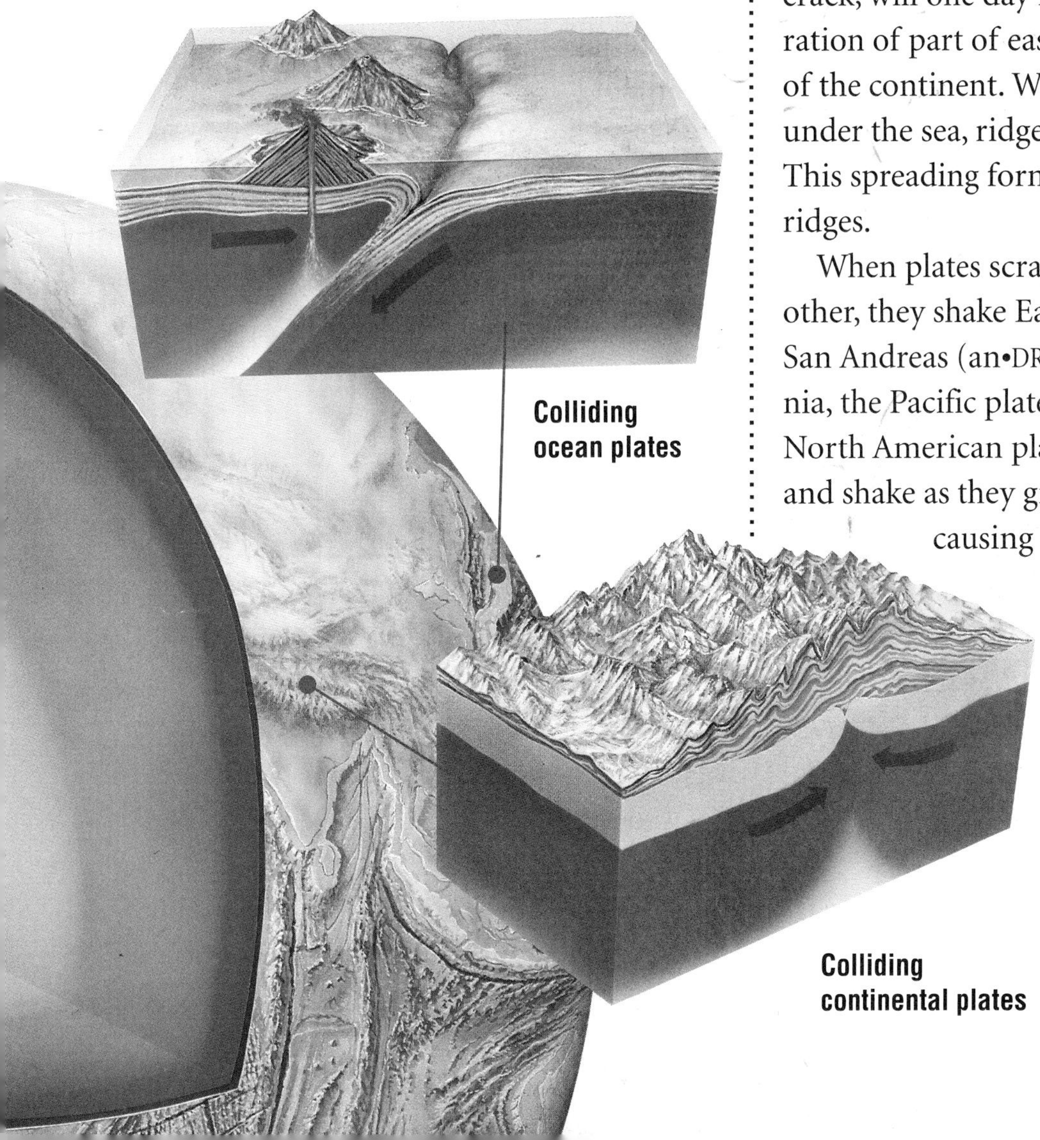

The Himalayas formed as the Indian plate pushed into the Eurasian plate. The plates are still pushing together, and the mountains are still getting taller.

Mountain Formation

Mountains are Earth's highest landforms. They form as the crust folds, cracks, and bends upward because of the movements of Earth's plates.

Most of the highest mountains form where continental plates collide. As the plates push together, their edges crumple and fold into mountains. The Himalayas (him•uh•LAY•uhz), Earth's highest mountain range, formed this way.

At some places, continental and oceanic plates collide. Because continental rock is lighter than seafloor rock, the continental plate moves up and over the oceanic plate. The Cascade Mountains, near the Pacific Ocean, formed this way.

Mountains do not form only at the edges, or boundaries, of plates. Some mountains form where pressure from movement at the boundaries pushes a block of rock upward. The Grand Tetons (TEE•tahnz) of Wyoming rise straight up from the flat land around them.

Plates that pull apart leave gaps between them. Magma bubbles up between the plates. **Magma** is hot, soft rock from Earth's mantle. Magma builds up along the cracks, forming long chains of mountains under the ocean. These mountains are called *mid-ocean ridges.* The Mid-Atlantic Ridge is Earth's longest mountain range. It separates the North American and Eurasian plates in the North Atlantic and the South American and African plates in the South Atlantic.

✔ **How do most of the highest mountains form?**

Volcanoes

You have read that most volcanoes form at plate boundaries. A **volcano** is a mountain formed by lava and ash. *Lava* is magma that reaches Earth's surface. *Ash* is small pieces of hardened lava.

Chains of volcanoes form where a continental plate and an oceanic plate collide. The edge of the oceanic plate pushes under the edge of the continental plate. The leading edge of the oceanic plate melts as it sinks deep into the mantle. The melted rock becomes magma that forces its way up between the plates. The volcanoes of the Cascades, such as Mount St. Helens, formed this way.

Sometimes volcanoes form in the middle of plates, over unusually hot columns of magma. The magma melts a hole in the plate and rises through the hole, causing a volcanic eruption. The Hawaiian Islands are the tops of a chain of volcanoes that formed in the middle of the Pacific plate. As the Pacific plate continues moving over this hot spot, new volcanoes and new islands form. The big island of Hawai'i, with its active volcano, Kīlauea, is the youngest island in the chain. Kure Atoll, an extinct volcano 2617 km (about 1625 mi) to the northwest, is the oldest.

✔ **What is a volcano?**

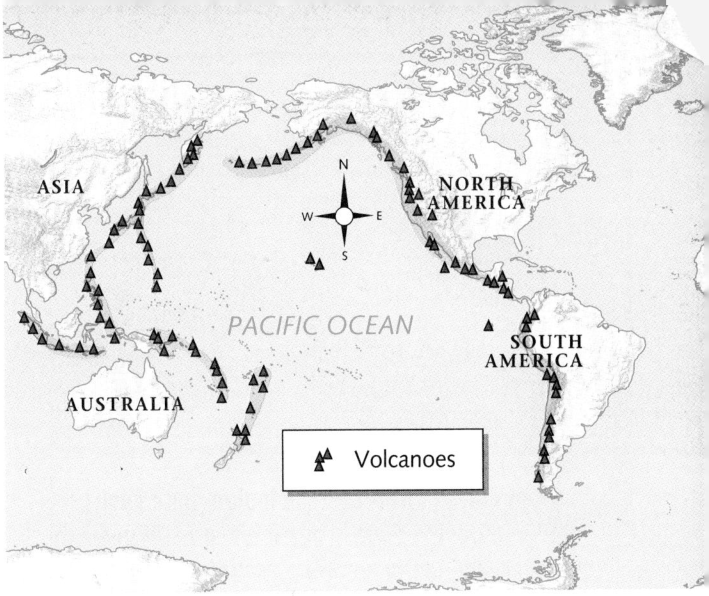

▲ **Many volcanoes are located at plate boundaries around the Pacific plate. That's why this area is called the Ring of Fire.**

THE INSIDE STORY

Volcanoes

Volcanoes take on their characteristic shapes as lava and ash build up around their openings, or *vents*.

Shield volcanoes are broad volcanoes with gentle slopes. They are mostly lava.

Cinder cone volcanoes are tall and narrow, with steep slopes. They are mostly ash.

Composite volcanoes are wide and have fairly steep slopes. They are lava and ash.

In 1964 a large earthquake hit Anchorage, Alaska. Streets split open, bridges collapsed, and houses slid downhill toward the sea.

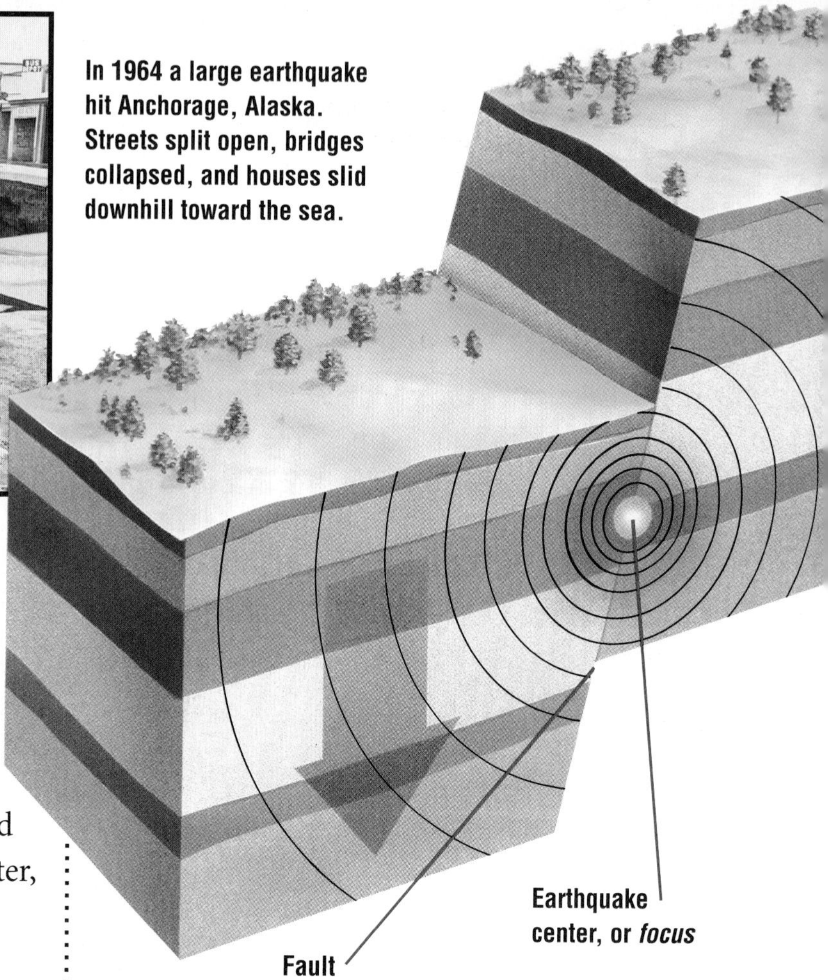

Earthquakes

On March 27, 1964, thousands of people in Anchorage, Alaska, were shaken as the ground rocked under them. A strong earthquake, possibly the most powerful one ever recorded, knocked down houses, broke up roads, and cut water, gas, and power lines all over the area.

An **earthquake** is a shaking of the ground caused by the sudden release of energy in Earth's crust. The energy released as plates crush together, scrape past each other, or bend along jagged boundaries can cause great damage. Earthquakes are very common. More than a million of them occur each year. However, most are too small to be felt or to cause damage.

Major Earthquakes

Magnitude	Year	Location
9.1	1964	Alaska
8.9	1933	Japan
8.4	1946	Japan
8.2	1976	China
8.1	1979	Indonesia
8.1	1985	Mexico
6.9	1989	California
6.8	1994	California

▲ The Richter scale is used to measure relative strengths, or *magnitudes,* of earthquakes. On this scale an earthquake with a magnitude of 7.5, for example, is 32 times more powerful than an earthquake with a magnitude of 6.5.

Many earthquakes occur along the boundaries of the Pacific plate. Earthquakes also occur along faults in the crust. You have read that Earth's crust can bend or break in the middle of a plate as forces press in on it. These breaks can form **faults**, or places where pieces of the crust move.

An earthquake sends out energy in the form of *seismic* (SYZ•mik) *waves.* Seismic waves are like ripples that form on a pond when a stone is tossed in. Scientists measure and record seismic waves on an instrument called a *seismograph* (SYZ•muh•graf). These measurements can then be used to compare the relative strengths of earthquakes.

✓ **What is an earthquake?**

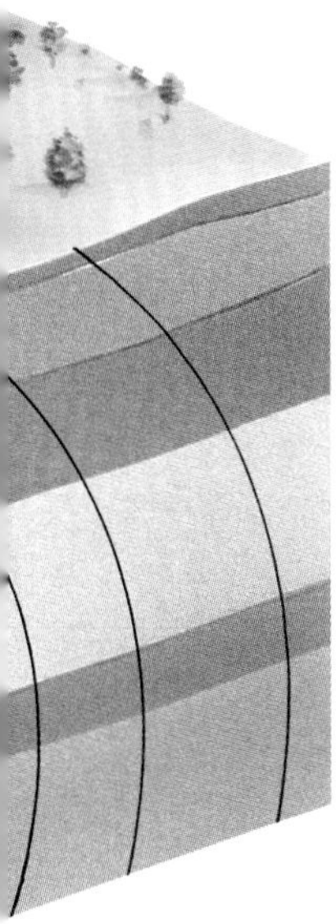

◄ Sudden movement along a fault can cause an earthquake.

Summary

Earth has three layers: the crust, the mantle, and the core. Rock of the crust and upper mantle makes up plates that fit together like puzzle pieces. Earth's plates collide, pull apart, and slide past each other. Most mountains and volcanoes form at plate boundaries. Many earthquakes also occur at plate boundaries.

Review

1. Describe three ways in which Earth's plates interact.
2. What is magma and where does it come from?
3. How do volcanoes form where oceanic and continental plates collide?
4. **Critical Thinking** Assume that the overall size of Earth's crust stays the same. If one plate is pushing away from the plate next to it on one side, what must be happening at the boundary with another plate on the opposite side?
5. **Test Prep** Many strong earthquakes are caused by —

   A plates sliding past each other
   B lava flowing down the side of a volcano
   C plates spreading apart
   D hot magma

LINKS

MATH LINK

Earthquake Magnitudes Each whole number on the Richter scale represents a force 32 times as strong as the next lower number. An earthquake of magnitude 7 is 32 times as strong as one of magnitude 6. How many times as strong is an earthquake of magnitude 8 compared with an earthquake of magnitude 5?

WRITING LINK

Informative Writing—Explanation The 1980 explosion of Mount St. Helens was a very powerful volcanic eruption. Find pictures in books and magazines of Mount St. Helens before, during, and after the eruption. Write captions for the pictures to explain what happened. Share your photo essay with your class.

LITERATURE LINK

Eruption: *Volcano: The Eruption and Healing of Mount St. Helens* by Patricia Lauber (Bradbury Press, 1986) explains how and why Mount St. Helens erupted. It also describes the destruction the eruption caused, and how the land has since recovered.

TECHNOLOGY LINK

Learn more about volcanoes by viewing *Ring of Fire* and *Volcano Hunters* on the **Harcourt Science Newsroom Video.**

CNN Turner Le@rning

LESSON 3

How Has Earth's Surface Changed?

In this lesson, you can . . .

INVESTIGATE the movement of continents.

LEARN ABOUT how Earth's surface has changed over time.

LINK to math, writing, fine arts, and technology.

◀ Over millions of years, these trees have turned to stone.

INVESTIGATE

Movement of the Continents

Activity Purpose Earth's surface 100 million years ago probably looked much different than it does today. In the last lesson, you read that Earth's surface is made up of plates that move. In this investigation, you will **make a model** to find out how Earth's surface might have looked before these plates moved to their present locations.

Materials

- 3 copies of a world map
- scissors
- 3 sheets of construction paper
- glue
- globe or world map

Activity Procedure

1. Cut out the continents from one copy of the world map.
2. Arrange the continents into one large "supercontinent" on a sheet of construction paper. As you would with a jigsaw puzzle, arrange them so their edges fit together as closely as possible. (Picture A)
3. Label the pieces with the names of their present continents, and glue them onto the paper.
4. Use a globe or world map to locate the following mountains: Cascades, Andes, Atlas, Himalayas, Alps. Then draw these mountains on the supercontinent.

Picture A

Picture B

5. Use your textbook to locate volcanoes and places where earthquakes have occurred. Put a *V* in places where you know there are volcanoes, such as the Cascades. Put an *E* in places where you know that earthquakes have occurred, such as western North America.
6. Repeat Steps 1–5 with the second copy of the world map, but before gluing the continents to the construction paper, separate them by about 2.5 cm. That is, leave about 2.5 cm of space between North America and Eurasia, between South America and Africa, and so on. (Picture B)
7. Glue the third world map copy onto a sheet of construction paper. Then place the three versions of the world map in order from the oldest to the youngest.

Draw Conclusions

1. Where do the continents fit together the best?
2. Where are most of the mountains, volcanoes, and earthquake sites in relation to the present continents? Why do you think they are there?
3. **Scientists at Work** Scientists **use models**, such as maps, to better understand complex structures and processes. How did your models of Earth's continents help you **draw conclusions** about Earth's past? What limitations did your models have?

Investigate Further **Hypothesize** about the fact that the continents do not fit together exactly. Then **plan and conduct a simple investigation** to test your hypothesis.

Process Skill Tip

It is impossible to actually see Earth's surface as it looked millions of years ago. But by **using a model**, you can **draw conclusions** about how it may have looked.

LEARN ABOUT

How Earth's Surface Has Changed

FIND OUT

- how Earth's surface features have changed over millions of years
- how fossils help scientists to learn about plants and animals of the past

VOCABULARY

continental drift
Pangea
fossil

Continental Drift

From evidence like the models you used in the investigation, scientists infer that Earth's surface has not always looked the way it does today. The surface is constantly changing because of continental drift. **Continental drift** is the theory of how Earth's continents move over its surface.

According to the theory, about 225 million years ago, all of the land on Earth was joined together in one "supercontinent" called **Pangea** (pan•JEE•uh). Evidence suggests that about 200 million years ago, Pangea broke into two big continents. The southern one, Gondwana, contained all the land that is now in the Southern Hemisphere. The northern continent, Laurasia, contained land that would become North America and Eurasia. Finally, Gondwana and Laurasia broke into smaller land masses, forming the continents we know today.

Since the continents are still moving, you might infer that the surface of Earth will be very different 200 million years from now. The Atlantic Ocean is getting wider, pushing Europe and North America apart. The Pacific Ocean is getting smaller. And Australia is moving north.

✔ **What is the theory of continental drift?**

Continental Drift

200 million years ago
Pangea begins to break apart.

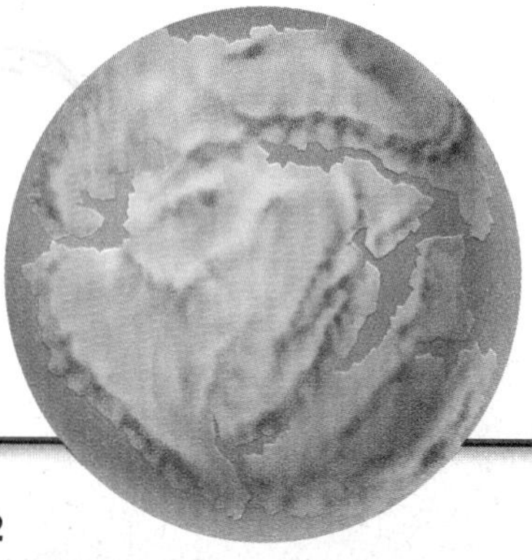

100 million years ago
Gondwana breaks into smaller continents earlier than Laurasia does.

Today
Earth's surface may look even different in the future.

The Rock Record

If you were floating down the Colorado River through the deepest part of the Grand Canyon, shown at the right, you would be looking up at layers of sedimentary rock nearly 2 billion years old! *Sedimentary rock* is rock formed from sediments that have cemented together. The Grand Canyon is a mile-deep slice into Earth's history, cutting through 20 different layers of sediment.

The sedimentary rocks of the canyon contain a fossil record of organisms from Earth's earliest history. **Fossils** are the remains or traces of past life found in sedimentary rock. Scientists study fossils to find out how life on Earth has changed.

Scientists also depend on the fact that some things will always be the same. Processes that produced features like the Grand Canyon are still occurring today. Running water still erodes sedimentary rock layers, and new layers of sedimentary rock are still forming.

From the position of sedimentary rock layers, scientists can infer the relative ages of the rocks. Younger rock layers are found on top of older rock layers. Some of the oldest rock layers on Earth are near the bottom of the Grand Canyon.

The walls of the Grand Canyon contain rock from only the earliest stages of Earth's history. Erosion has worn away more recent rock. If you stand on the canyon's north rim, you are standing on rock that is about 250 million years old.

✔ **Why is looking at the Grand Canyon like looking at Earth's history?**

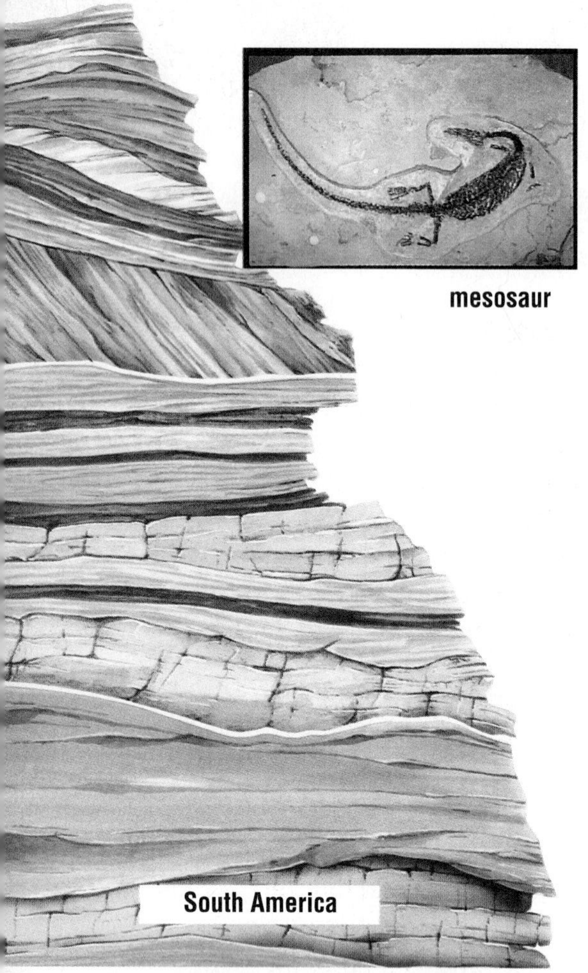

Similar rock layers and similar fossils have been found in both South America and Africa. This provides evidence that the continents may once have been joined together.

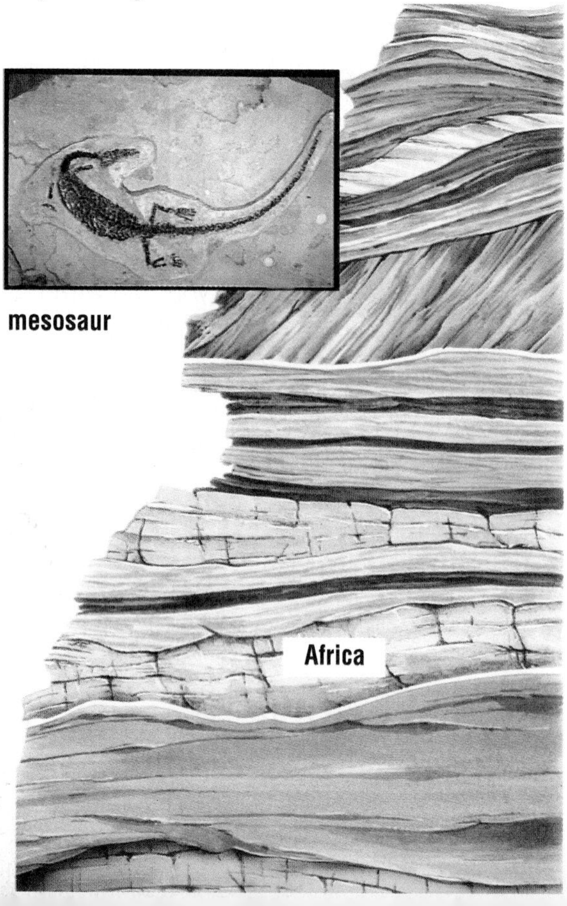

How Fossils Show Changes

Fossils show us that life on Earth has not always been the same as it is now. Dinosaurs once roamed Earth, as did large, elephantlike animals called *woolly mammoths.* Scientists have drawn conclusions about these creatures from what they left behind—whole mammoths frozen in ice and fossilized bones and teeth of dinosaurs.

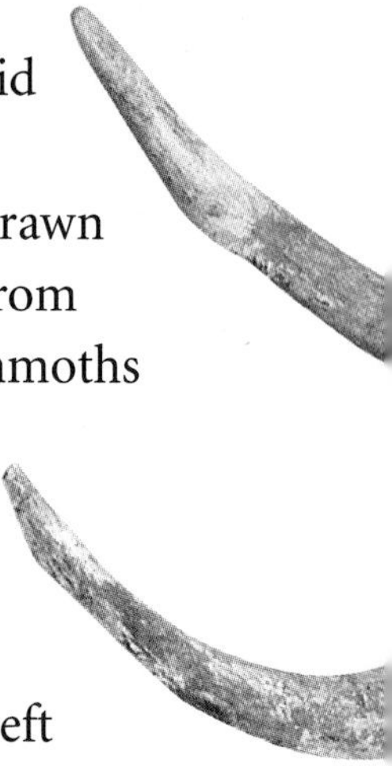

Most fossils, however, are not the actual remains of once-living organisms. Instead, they are traces left behind when dead plants and animals decayed or dissolved. When sediment buries an organism, it can produce a mold or cast as the sediment hardens into rock. A mold forms when underground water dissolves the organism, leaving only its shape behind in the rock. If minerals fill the empty space and harden, the fossil becomes a cast—like a dinosaur egg.

In addition to showing what kinds of organisms lived on Earth long ago, fossils also show that Earth's surface was different than it is today. Scientists have found fossils of sea organisms in rock at the tops of high mountains. They infer that those areas were once under water.

Scientists use fossil evidence to support the theory of continental drift. Fossils of similar plants and animals have been found in Africa, South America, India, and Australia. This means that these widely separated continents must have been joined at one time.

✔ **How are fossils used to show changes?**

▲ Scientists called *paleontologists* study fossils to learn about life of the past.

Summary

Earth's continents once were joined to form a supercontinent called Pangea. Pangea broke apart and, over millions of years, the continents drifted to their present locations. Fossils, the remains and traces of dead organisms, show what Earth's life was like in the past. They also show that Earth's surface has changed.

Review

1. What was Pangea?
2. How old are the oldest rocks of the Grand Canyon?
3. How do we know that Earth's life was different in the past?
4. **Critical Thinking** Why is the Grand Canyon important to scientists studying Earth's past?
5. **Test Prep** The Southern continent that existed 200 million years ago was called —

   A Gondwana
   B Precambria
   C Laurasia
   D Eurasia

LINKS

MATH LINK

Geologic Time Scale Research Earth's history. Then make a chart showing the relative lengths of the various eras and periods. Your chart should show how long each era and period lasted and how long ago each occurred. Draw the chart to scale. For example, if an era lasted for half the time of Earth's history, it should cover half the chart.

WRITING LINK

Informative Writing—Compare and Contrast You learned that Earth's continents were once in different places. Where will they be in the future? Research what a map of the world might look like 100 million years from now. Then compare and contrast this map with a current map in a report for your teacher.

ART LINK

Past Life Look for illustrations of what Earth's surface might have looked like thousands, or even millions, of years ago. Compare what you find with the way Earth's surface looks today.

TECHNOLOGY LINK

Learn more about changes to Earth's surface by visiting the National Air and Space Museum Internet site.
www.si.edu/harcourt/science

Smithsonian Institution®

Exploring Earth's Surface from Space

Newly released satellite images of the ocean floor are making scientists question old theories about the processes that change Earth's surface.

Satellite Secrets

Until recently, information collected by a U.S. government Geosat satellite was top secret. Now data gathered by this satellite has been released, and geologists are excited. However, they say it will take about ten years to analyze the satellite's images of Earth's geologic processes.

If you've ever sailed on the ocean, you probably couldn't tell that the water bulges up in certain places. It does this because of gravity. Rock on the ocean floor has a gravitational pull for the water around it. The more rock, the stronger the pull. The stronger the pull, the more the water bulges up. A 2000-m (about 6562-ft) underwater volcano causes a water bulge of about 2 m (6.6 ft).

Many of the volcanoes under the Pacific Ocean were discovered by gravity imaging.

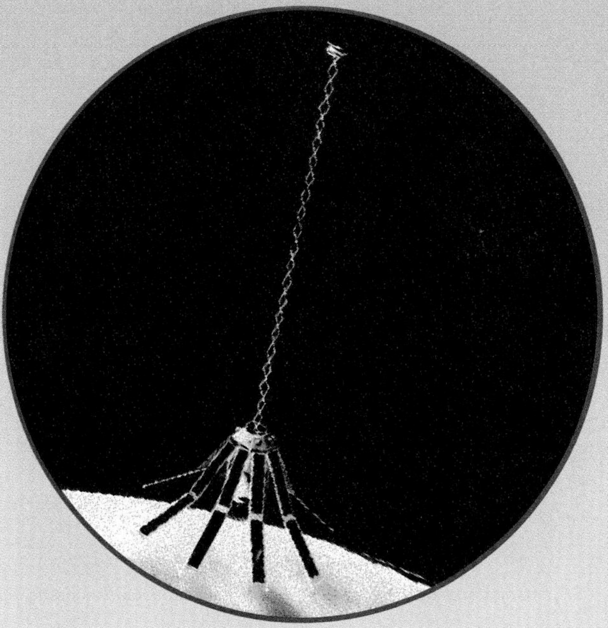

This drawing shows a Geosat circling Earth.

Sensitive equipment on board a Geosat can measure these bulges from space. By measuring the surface of the ocean very precisely, the satellite produces clear gravity images of volcanoes, mountain ranges, plains, and other "landforms" on the ocean floor.

New Data Shakes Up Old Theories

Many areas of the ocean floor had never been surveyed before. About half of the underwater volcanoes shown by the Geosat's gravity imaging had not been known to exist. Gravity images of water bulges are also making scientists question old theories about how volcanic island chains form.

The old theory, called the "hot spot" model, said that there are hot areas in Earth's mantle. As Earth's plates pass slowly over a hot spot, a long line of volcanoes forms. Each new volcano in the line is younger than the one just before it.

But the hot spot model can't explain some of the newly discovered volcano chains. For example, the Pukapuka Ridges, which extend for thousands of kilometers east of Tahiti, seem to have erupted all at the same time. Rock samples from different parts of the chain are all the same age.

Scientists are arguing about what these new discoveries mean in terms of the old theories about hot spots being correct. Many agree that the hot spot model may be wrong. All agree that there is much work ahead to develop more accurate theories based on this Geosat data.

THINK ABOUT IT

1. How does gravity imaging work?
2. Why do you think oil companies might be interested in gravity images?

WEB LINK:
For science and technology updates, visit The Learning Site. www.harcourtschool.com

Careers Satellite Technician

What They Do
Satellite technicians work as part of a team that plans, constructs, launches, and operates satellites. They may also work at control stations to receive and monitor data transmissions from satellites.

Education and Training A person wishing to become a satellite technician needs training in electronics, computer sciences, and communications systems.

PEOPLE IN SCIENCE

Kia K. Baptist

GEOSCIENTIST

"A key to being a scientist is to be unafraid to ask questions and unafraid that there may not be answers."

Kia Baptist can see what lies below Earth's surface. She is a geoscientist who works for an oil company. Her job is to help find oil and natural gas resources by finding clues in different kinds of data.

Ms. Baptist collects seismic data by creating small "earthquakes" in rock. Then she analyzes the sound signals that return and uses them to map the rock formations and structures underground.

Ms. Baptist also analyzes geochemical data to learn the chemical nature of the rock. This tells her what kind of rock it is, how old it is, and whether there is oil present. This information, along with computer technology, allows her to give advice to the oil companies on specific locations where oil and natural gas may be found.

Sedimentary rock layers

Looking for clues is natural for Ms. Baptist. As a child growing up in Baltimore, Maryland, she was a mystery solver. She decided she wanted to help solve the mysteries of space by becoming an astronaut. Several times she worked as an intern at NASA, learning all she could about astronomy and physics. She took courses in many areas of science, believing that knowing about all branches of science would help her do her best work in one. When she began to study geology and chemistry, she realized her true interest lay in those areas. She hasn't stopped studying the Earth since then.

Ms. Baptist gives good advice to young scientists. She says, "Part of the process of science is attacking a problem and trying to find answers, but don't be intimidated if you don't find answers right away. Just keep learning."

THINK ABOUT IT

1. How could analyzing seismic data give clues about where oil is located?
2. Why is it important to know the specific location of oil?

Model Earth

How can you model Earth's layers?

Materials

- rounded objects, such as

an apple	a tennis ball
an avocado	an orange
a peach	a plum
a hard-boiled egg	plain chocolates, or
a nectarine	chocolate-covered peanuts

Procedure

1. Make two columns on a sheet of paper.
2. Label one column "Does Model Earth's Layers." Label the other column "Does Not Model Earth's Layers."
3. Decide what characteristics an object must have to model Earth's layers.
4. Examine each object. Then write the name of the object in the appropriate column.

Draw Conclusions

What characteristics must an object have to model Earth's layers? Which parts of the objects in the "Does Model Earth's Layers" column represent Earth's layers? What other objects can you think of that model Earth's layers?

Featuring Earth

How do landforms change?

Materials

- apple
- tape measure
- pan
- hotpad
- oven

Procedure

1. Measure the circumference of the apple.
2. Place the apple in a pan and, using the hot pad, put the pan in the oven and bake it for one hour at 300°F.

3. Your teacher or another adult will remove the apple from the oven. Allow it to cool, and measure it again.
4. Observe the features of the baked apple.

Draw Conclusions

In some ways, baked apples are a good model of how Earth's landforms change. Compare the circumference of the apple before and after you baked it. What happened to the peel as the apple cooled? What layer of Earth does the peel represent? What "landforms" can you identify on the apple peel? In what ways is the apple *not* a good model of Earth's changing landforms?

Chapter 1 Review and Test Preparation

Vocabulary Review

Use the terms below to complete the sentences. The page numbers in ( ) tell you where to look in the chapter if you need help.

landform (C6)
weathering (C7)
erosion (C7)
deposition (C7)
mass movement (C9)
crust (C14)
mantle (C14)
core (C14)
plate (C15)
magma (C16)
volcano (C16)
earthquake (C18)
fault (C18)
continental drift (C22)
Pangea (C22)
fossils (C23)

1. An ____ is a sudden release of energy in Earth's ____, causing the ground to shake.
2. A rigid block of Earth's crust and upper mantle rock is a ____.
3. A ____ is a physical feature on Earth's surface, such as a mountain or valley.
4. The remains or traces of past life found in Earth's crust are called ____.
5. Hot, soft rock from Earth's mantle is ____.
6. A ____ is a break in Earth's crust, along which pieces of the crust move.
7. ____ is the process of breaking rock into soil, sand, and other particles called sediment.
8. Lava is magma that reaches Earth's surface through an opening, called a ____, in Earth's crust.
9. The downhill movement of rock and soil because of gravity is ____.
10. The ____ is the layer of rock beneath Earth's crust.
11. The theory that the continents move over Earth's surface is ____.
12. ____ is the supercontinent that held all of Earth's land 225 million years ago.
13. ____ is the process of moving sediment from one place to another, and ____ is the process of dropping, or depositing, sediment in a new location.
14. The ____ is the center of Earth.

Connect Concepts

Use the Word Bank to complete the sentences.

deltas **beaches** **tables** **sinkholes** **terminal moraines**
arches **canyons** **dunes** **floodplains**

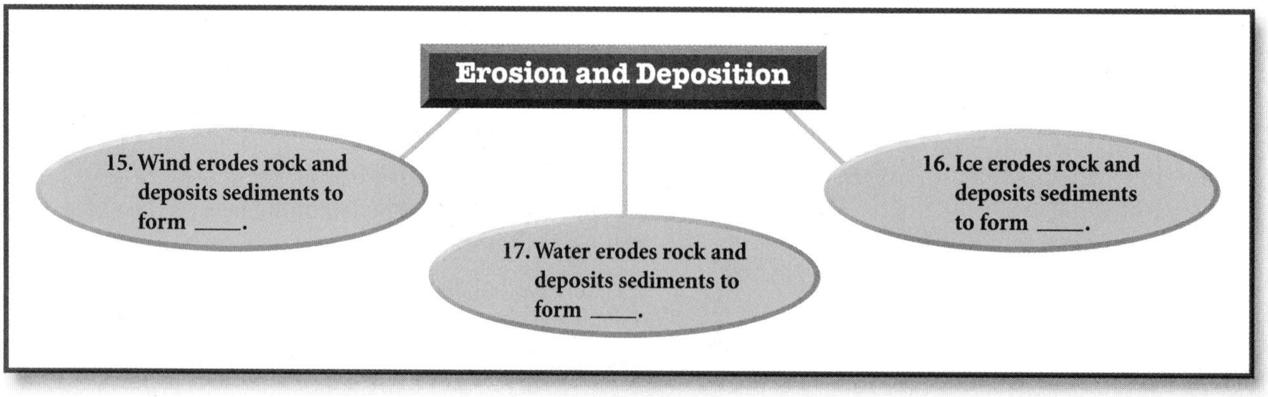

Check Understanding

Write the letter of the best choice.

18. Beginning with the outermost layer, Earth's layers are the —

A crust, magma, and core
B crust, mantle, and core
C core, mantle, and crust
D core, magma, and crust

19. Gondwana and Laurasia were formed by —

F continental drift
G erosion
H deposition
J earthquakes

20. Which of the following was **NOT** an ancient continent?

A Pangea
B Laurasia
C Gondwana
D Cenozoa

Critical Thinking

21. Explain why water erodes Earth's surface more than wind does.

22. If the mantle were solid rock, what feature would not form on Earth's surface? Explain.

23. Scientists have found many fossils of past life. Are fossils still being formed today? Explain.

Process Skills Review

24. What can you **observe** about these pieces of rock that shows you which one has been weathered and moved by water?

25. How might you **make a model** of a volcano?

Performance Assessment

Plate Boundaries

Identify the three types of plate boundaries at A, B, and C in the illustration below. Explain what is happening at each boundary.

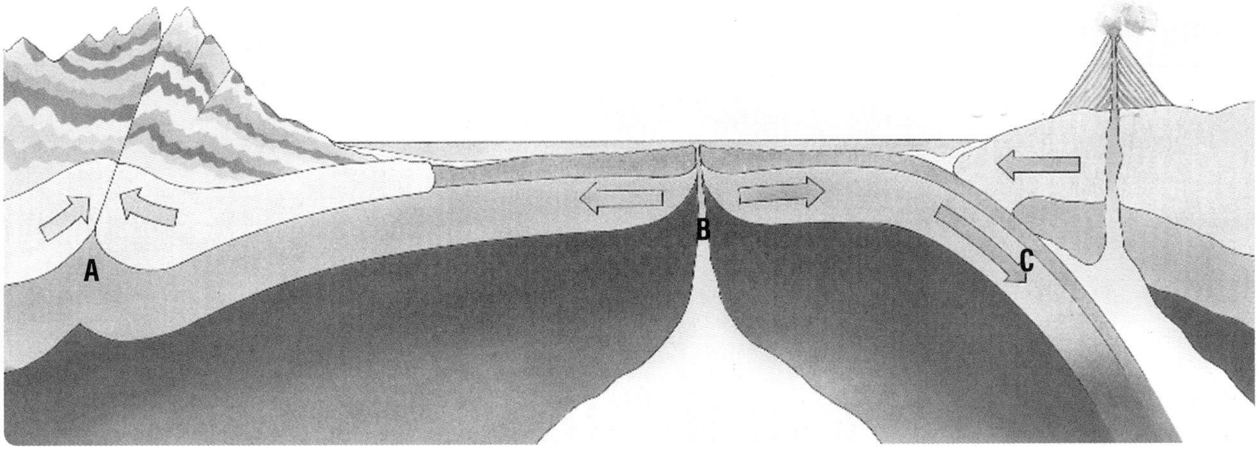

Chapter 2

Renewable and Nonrenewable Resources

Can you picture what life would be like if there were no oil or coal? How would people drive their cars or make electricity? Coal and oil are natural resources that people use for energy.

FAST FACT

More than three-fourths of the energy we use comes from fossil fuels (natural gas, coal, and petroleum). Less than four percent comes from inexhaustible energy sources, such as the sun, the wind, or the ocean tides.

Energy Sources

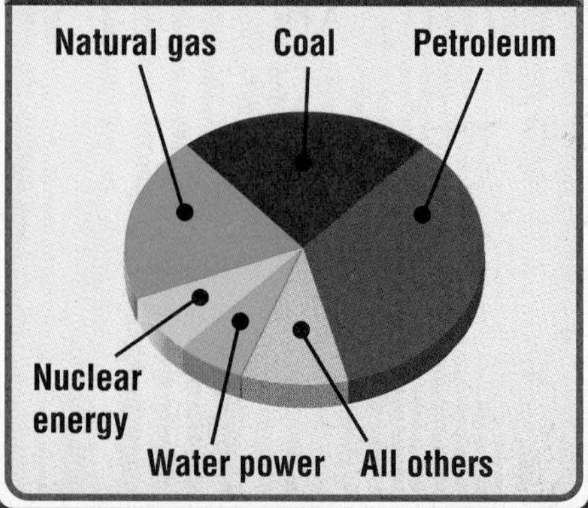

Vocabulary Preview

- natural resource
- nonrenewable resource
- renewable resource
- reusable resource
- fossil fuels
- natural gas
- peat
- lignite
- bitumen
- anthracite
- recycling

FAST FACT

Recycling cans, as shown here, saves electricity as well as aluminum. You can run a television for four hours with the electricity it takes to produce one aluminum can.

FAST FACT

In 1900 there were 8000 cars in the United States. Twenty years later there were more than 8,000,000. Today there are about 150,000,000 cars.

LESSON 1

What Are Natural Resources?

In this lesson, you can . . .

INVESTIGATE the properties of minerals.

LEARN ABOUT Earth's natural resources.

LINK to math, writing, technology, and other areas.

Color is just one of the physical properties of minerals. ▼

▲ Quartz
▼ Pyrite

INVESTIGATE

Properties of Minerals

Activity Purpose Minerals have physical properties, or characteristics. Minerals can be hard or soft. Some are magnetic. Minerals such as quartz can form beautiful crystals. The properties of minerals make them useful to people for various purposes. In this investigation you will **observe** minerals. Then you will **make predictions** about their properties.

Materials

- 6 mineral samples (talc, pyrite, quartz, fluorite, magnetite, graphite)
- tile
- magnet

Activity Procedure

1. Make a copy of the chart below. List the names of the minerals your teacher gives you.
2. **Observe** each mineral. **Predict** which one will be the hardest. Then rub the minerals against each other to test their hardness. A harder mineral will scratch a softer one. Under *Hardness* on the chart, write a number from 1 to 6 for the hardness of each mineral. Use 1 for the softest mineral and 6 for the hardest mineral.

Mineral	Hardness	Shine	Streak	Magnetic
talc				
pyrite				
quartz				
fluorite				
magnetite				
graphite				

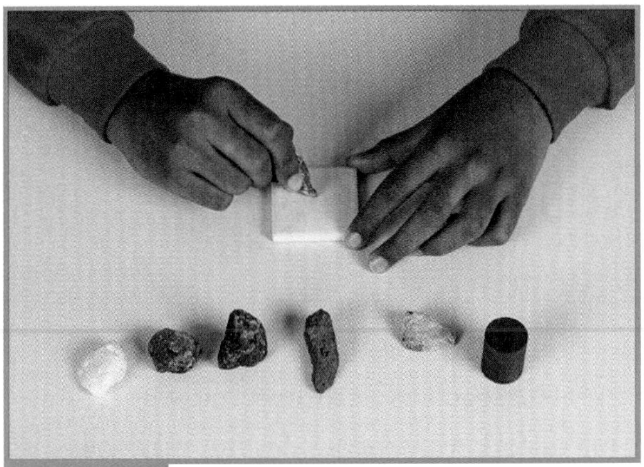

Picture A

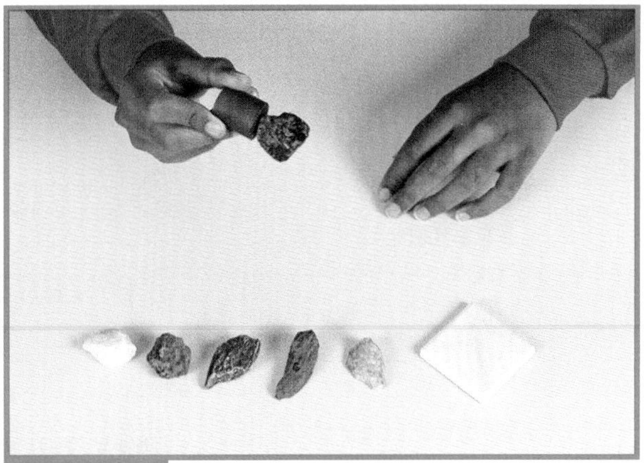

Picture B

3. **Observe** each mineral, and decide whether or not it is shiny. Write *yes* next to the name of the mineral if it is shiny. Write *no* if it is not.

4. Now **predict** the color of the streak each mineral will make. A streak is the colored line a mineral makes when it is rubbed on a tile. Then rub each mineral on the tile. If the mineral makes a streak, write the color of the streak next to the mineral's name. Write *none* if the mineral does not make a streak. (Picture A)

5. Finally, **predict** which minerals will be attracted to a magnet. Test each mineral with a magnet. Write *yes* next to the names of minerals that stick to the magnet. Write *no* next to the names of those that do not. (Picture B)

Draw Conclusions

1. Which mineral is the softest? **Compare** your test results with your predictions.
2. Which minerals make streaks? **Compare** your test results with your color predictions.
3. Which minerals are magnetic? **Compare** your test results with your predictions.
4. **Scientists at Work** Scientists often **predict** what might happen. How did careful observations of the mineral samples help you make better predictions about their properties?

Investigate Further Use the information you gathered on each mineral's properties to **infer** its uses.

Process Skill Tip

Before you **predict,** make careful observations. This makes your prediction better than a simple guess.

LEARN ABOUT

Natural Resources

FIND OUT

- what natural resources are
- why some natural resources might get used up

VOCABULARY

natural resource
nonrenewable resource
renewable resource
reusable resource

Nonrenewable Resources

In the investigation you learned that minerals have many physical properties. Properties such as hardness and shine make minerals useful for different purposes. Useful minerals and other materials that people take from the Earth are called **natural resources**.

In the past hundred years, people have been using natural resources at a faster rate than ever before. That has made scientists wonder whether some natural resources may one day be completely used up. A resource that cannot be replaced once it is used up is called a **nonrenewable resource**. Nonrenewable resources take thousands of years to form. Once they are used up, they are, as a practical matter, gone.

Rock and mineral resources are nonrenewable. We use rock resources to construct buildings and roads. The silicon chips that make a computer work come from minerals. So does the "lead," or graphite, in a pencil. Other mineral resources are

The aluminum in the basketball backboard comes from the mineral bauxite. ▶

Our bodies need mineral resources. Foods such as fruits and vegetables take minerals from the soil.

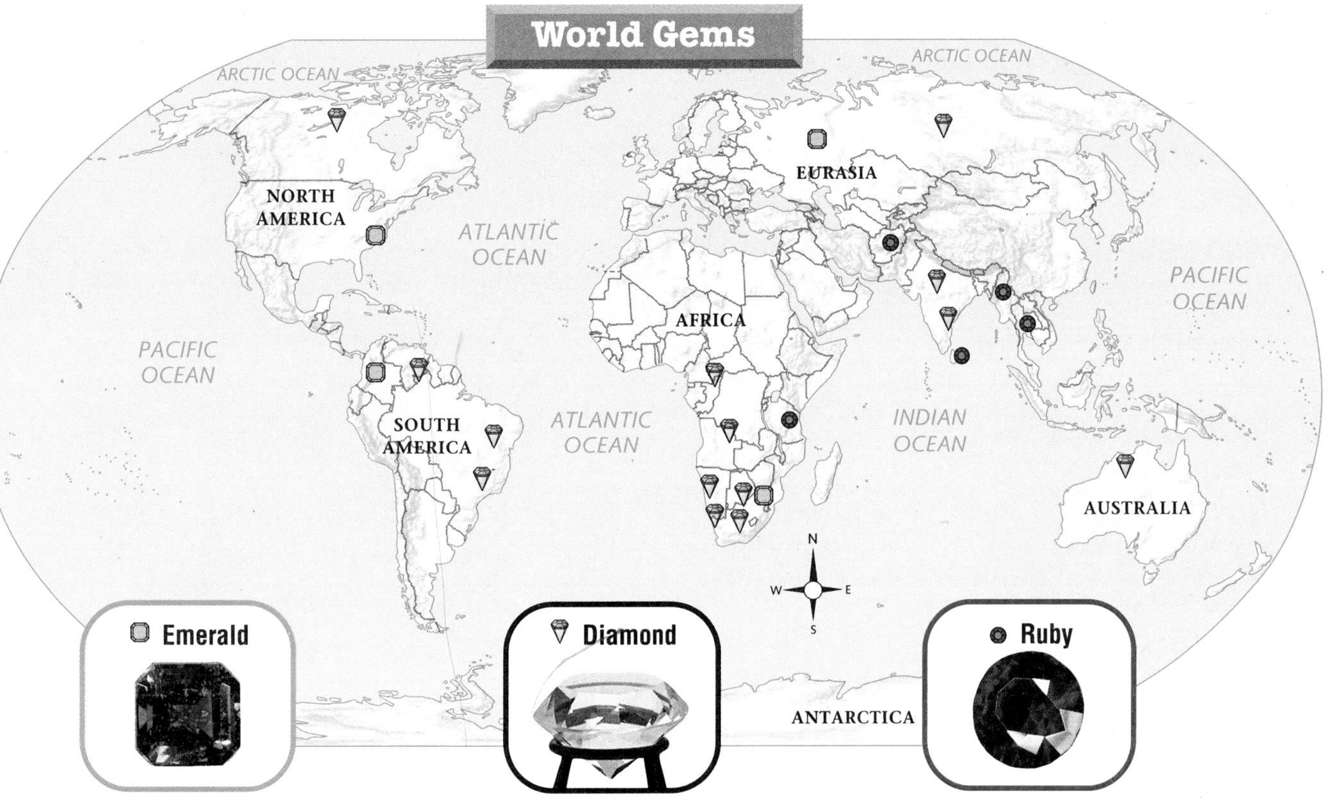

▲ Gems are rare and valuable minerals. Some parts of the world have large deposits of certain gems.

▲ Many buildings are made of granite. Granite is used for buildings because it is hard, and its surface can be polished.

▲ Limestone is also an important building material. It is used to make the concrete for this basketball court.

necessary for the production of metals such as aluminum, iron, copper, silver, and gold. And gems—such as diamonds, rubies, and emeralds—are minerals, too.

Any rock containing a large amount of a mineral is called a *mineral deposit.* Mineral deposits form in several ways. Some minerals dissolve in hot water. As the hot mineral solution flows through cracks in cooler rocks, some minerals fall out of solution and form deposits called *veins.* Gold, copper, and silver are found in veins.

Mineral deposits can also form in magma. As magma cools, heavy minerals sink, forming deposits rich in metals such as iron and nickel.

Mineral deposits are distributed unevenly in the Earth. Some nations have many mineral resources, while other nations have few. Nations usually trade with each other to get the resources they need.

Soil is another nonrenewable resource. All the Earth's forests and food crops take minerals out of the soil as they grow. Minerals go back into the soil when plants and animals die and decay. But people can destroy soil by overusing it, or by putting certain chemicals on it. Overusing soil removes more minerals than decay can put back. And some chemicals can poison soil so that nothing will grow. Losing soil is a major problem, because it takes thousands of years for even a few centimeters of soil to be replaced.

✔ **What are nonrenewable resources?**

Renewable and Reusable Resources

The Earth produces new amounts of some natural resources at the same rate as they are used. A **renewable resource** is a resource that is replaced as it is used.

Most forests, for example, are renewable resources, but only if enough new trees are allowed to grow. Important products, such as lumber, paper, cardboard, tar, and turpentine, come from forests. When humans cut down trees, new ones can grow in their place. If large areas of an old forest are cut at one time, however, the new forest may have different kinds of plants and animals than the old forest did. Some animals need the plants of the old forest for food or shelter. Without those plants the animals might not survive.

Resources such as water and air are not renewable, but they can be used over and over. A **reusable resource** is a natural resource that can be used more than once. Reusable resources are sometimes called *inexhaustible resources.* Natural cycles renew the Earth's reusable resources. The water cycle, for example, allows Earth's limited supply of fresh water to be used over and over again. Heat from the sun evaporates water from the Earth's surface—mainly from the oceans—into the atmosphere. As air cools, water vapor condenses, forming clouds. Water then falls back to Earth from clouds as rain or snow.

Although reusable resources cannot be used up, they can be polluted. During evaporation, water loses any pollution it may have picked up. However, rain and snow pick up any pollution in the air. Acid rain, for example, falls where cloud drops mix with certain chemical pollutants in the air.

✔ **What is a renewable resource?**

Some resources—air, forests, and water—can last forever if they are used carefully.

Summary

Natural resources are useful materials that people take from the Earth. Resources such as soil, rocks, and minerals are nonrenewable. Once they are used up, they cannot be replaced. Some resources—such as forests, water, and air—are renewable or reusable.

Review

1. What is a renewable resource?
2. What is a reusable resource?
3. List two types of nonrenewable resources.
4. **Critical Thinking** What would happen if resources such as air and water could not be reused?
5. **Test Prep** Which of the following is a reusable resource?
   A quartz
   B water
   C a tree
   D iron

LINKS

MATH LINK

Recycling It takes about 100 recycled aluminum cans to make 90 new cans. If your school has a party, and 375 aluminum cans are returned for recycling, how many new cans can be made?

WRITING LINK

Informative Writing—Compare and Contrast Write a paragraph for a younger student explaining the differences between renewable, nonrenewable, and inexhaustible resources. Use examples in your explanation.

SOCIAL STUDIES LINK

Resource Map Choose a mineral resource that is found in the United States, such as copper or iron. Make a map of the United States showing where this resource is found.

PHYSICAL EDUCATION LINK

PE Resources How many products made from natural resources are used during PE class? Look around during the class, and then make a list.

TECHNOLOGY LINK

Learn more about mineral resources by viewing *River of Gold* on the **Harcourt Science Newsroom Video.**

CNN Turner Le@rning

LESSON 2

How Do Fossil Fuels Form?

In this lesson, you can . . .

INVESTIGATE storage rocks.

LEARN ABOUT how fossil fuels form.

LINK to math, writing, technology, and other areas.

This tower separates petroleum into products such as asphalt, heating oil, and gasoline. ▼

INVESTIGATE

What Kinds of Rocks Store Petroleum

Activity Purpose Petroleum is one of the most important fuel resources in the United States. The petroleum that people use today came from the decay of ancient sea life. The remains of microscopic organisms settled to the sea floor and became part of the ocean sediments. In time, the sediments changed to rock. It was within this *source rock* that the decaying organisms slowly changed into petroleum. The pressure of additional sediments squeezed the petroleum out of the source rock and into layers called *storage rock*. In this investigation you will **use numbers** to **compare** rocks and determine which is the best storage rock.

Materials

- limestone
- sandstone
- shale
- paper plates
- dropper
- mineral oil
- clock

Activity Procedure

1. Place the rock samples on separate paper plates. **Observe** each rock. **Predict** which will be the best storage rock.
2. Fill the dropper with mineral oil. Put 5 drops of oil on the limestone sample. (Picture A)

Picture A

Picture B

3. **Observe** and **record** the time it takes for the 5 drops of oil to soak into the limestone.

4. Continue adding oil, counting the drops, until the limestone will hold no more oil. **Record** the number of drops it takes. (Picture B)

5. Repeat Steps 2–4 with the other rock samples.

Draw Conclusions

1. Which rock soaked up the oil the fastest? What was the time?
2. Which rock soaked up the most oil? What was the number of drops?
3. Which rock is the best storage rock? Explain.
4. **Scientists at Work** Scientists often **use numbers** to **compare** things. How did you use numbers to compare the oil-storing ability of the rocks?

Investigate Further How could you determine which of the rocks is a source rock for petroleum? **Plan a simple investigation** to answer this question. Then decide what equipment you would need to carry out this investigation.

Process Skill Tip

You can **use numbers** to do many things. You can solve math problems, count objects, put things in order, or **compare** one thing with another. In this activity you compared the oil-storing ability of certain rocks.

LEARN ABOUT

How Fossil Fuels Form

FIND OUT

- the types of fossil fuels
- how fossil fuels form

VOCABULARY

fossil fuels
natural gas
peat
lignite
bitumen
anthracite

Fossil Fuels

Coal, natural gas, and petroleum are valuable resources known as **fossil fuels.** They are called *fossil* fuels because they formed from the remains of once-living organisms. Fossil fuels are nonrenewable resources.

Burning a fossil fuel releases large amounts of energy. That's one reason why people use fossil fuels more than any other energy source on Earth. Another reason is that fossil fuels are found in many places. In the last hundred years, the technology for finding fossil fuels has improved. This has increased the use of fossil fuels.

Fossil fuels are also important resources for making other products. For example, coal is used to make steel. And many chemicals, called petrochemicals, are made from petroleum. Petrochemicals are used to produce medicines, makeup, paints, and plastics.

✔ **What are fossil fuels?**

Many energy stations burn coal to produce electricity. ▼

A lot of the items you use every day are made of chemicals that come from petroleum. ▼

Almost all cars, trucks, and buses run on fuel made from petroleum. ▼

Miners travel deep into the Earth to dig coal from underground layers, or seams. ►

Energy from the Sun

Burning fossil fuels releases energy that came from the sun. The energy was stored in the bodies of ancient organisms that were buried in sediments millions of years ago. So coal, natural gas, and petroleum are found in layers of sedimentary rock.

Petroleum is the world's most widely used fossil fuel. It produces a lot of heat when it is burned. Petroleum is used mainly for transportation, because it is easier to store and transport than coal and natural gas.

The petroleum used today formed when microorganisms died and fell to the bottoms of ancient seas. Over many years, layer upon layer of sediment covered them. Deep within the Earth, where there is a lot of heat and pressure, the organic matter of their decayed bodies slowly turned into petroleum and natural gas.

Natural gas is mostly a gas called *methane*. It is usually found with petroleum. Natural gas is used mostly for heating and cooking.

Coal is the most common fossil fuel. Much of the coal used today comes from plants that lived in swamps millions of years ago. As these plants died, they sank to the bottoms of the swamps. Mud and other sediments covered their remains, and slowly the plants changed into coal.

The United States has large deposits of fossil fuels, especially coal and natural gas. But the United States uses so much petroleum that some is imported from places such as Saudi Arabia and Nigeria.

Electric energy stations use most of the coal mined in the United States. Years ago, burning coal produced clouds of black smoke. Today, stations that burn coal have ways to control pollution.

The world is slowly running out of fossil fuels. To conserve fuel resources, many nations are trying to cut down on their use of these fuels. They are beginning to use energy sources that are inexhaustible—wind, solar, and hydroelectric energy.

✔ **Where did the energy in fossil fuels come from originally?**

Fossil Fuel Deposits

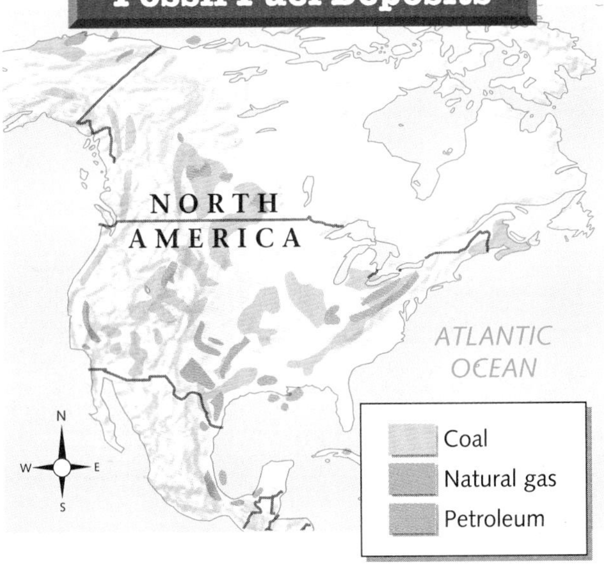

Coal Formation

As coal forms, it goes through four steps, or stages. At each stage the amount of carbon it contains increases. The first stage is the formation of peat. **Peat** is a soft, brown material made up of partly decayed plants. It forms as dead plants build up in swamps. Today some swamps and bogs, which are areas of wet and spongy ground, have deep layers of peat.

The second stage of coal formation produces lignite. **Lignite** (LIG•nyt) is a soft, brown rock. It forms as layers of sand and mud cover peat. As the layers build up, the pressure of their weight squeezes moisture out of the peat, turning it into a soft rock.

THE INSIDE STORY

Coal Formation

Peat can be found in marshy areas in Great Britain, Russia, and Ukraine. Some people dig out the peat and use it for heating and cooking. Burning peat produces a lot of smoke and pollutants. ▼

Most lignite mines are in eastern European countries. Lignite produces a lot of smoke when it is burned, but it doesn't provide much heat. ▼

Over millions of years, this pressure, along with heat from inside the Earth, turns peat into lignite.

Bitumen is the third stage of coal formation. **Bitumen** (bih•TOO•muhn) is a fairly hard, dark brown or black rock. Millions of years of heat and the weight of even more layers of sediment turn lignite into bitumen. Bitumen is the most common type of coal mined and used today.

In the fourth stage, bitumen becomes anthracite. **Anthracite** (AN•thruh•syt) is a hard, black rock. Anthracite forms under great heat and pressure. It is almost pure carbon.

✔ **What are the four stages of coal formation?**

Most of the coal that is mined and used today is bitumen. As with lignite, burning bitumen produces a lot of smoke, but it also produces a lot of heat. ▼

There isn't much anthracite anywhere in the world. When it is burned, anthracite produces a lot of heat and very little smoke. Because of this, it is the most valuable form of coal. ▼

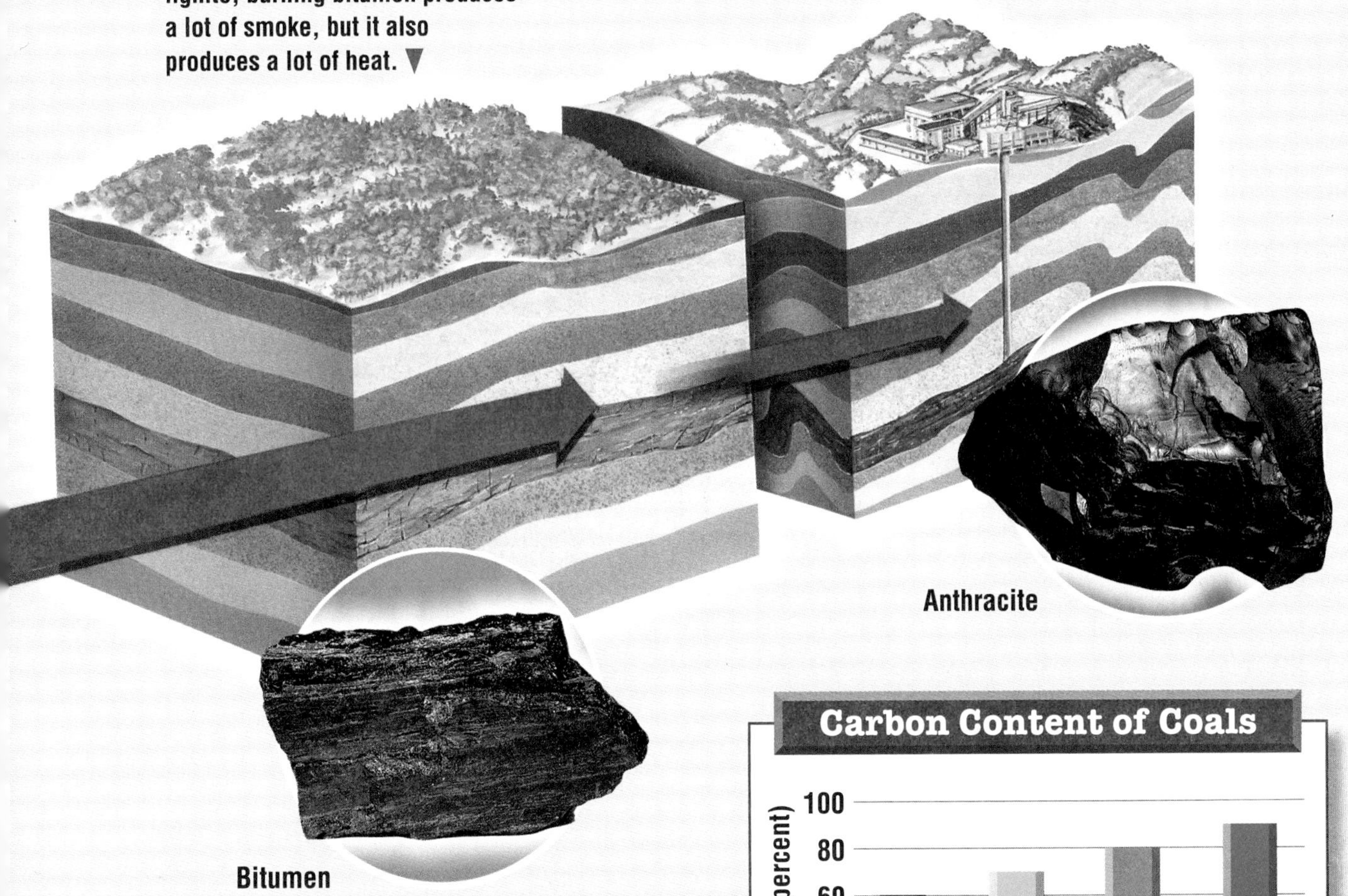

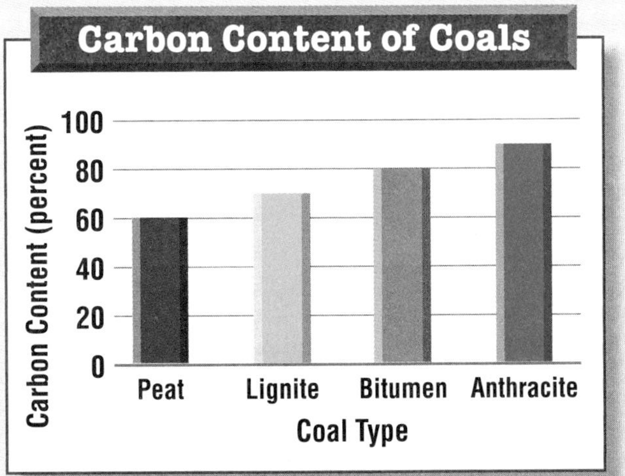

Petroleum and Natural Gas

Petroleum and natural gas are found only in sedimentary rock. Almost 60 percent of the world's supply is in sandstone. The rest is in limestone and other porous rocks. Geologists can identify rock structures that are likely to hold petroleum and natural gas, so they know where to look for these resources.

Since the microorganisms that formed them lived in seas, many petroleum and natural gas deposits are found under water. Underwater drilling takes place from huge platforms built over the water. In the United States these platforms are located in the Gulf of Mexico and off the California coast.

Some deposits of petroleum and natural gas are under land, in places that were once shallow seas. Drilling for these deposits occurs in California, Texas, Alaska, and other states.

When a drill locates a deposit of petroleum or natural gas, the petroleum has to be pumped from the ground. Natural gas comes out by itself. If there is not enough petroleum in one area to be pumped out directly, hot water or steam is forced into the deposit through a nearby well. This forces the petroleum, which is lighter than water, to the surface.

Sometimes the petroleum is under such great pressure that it gushes to the surface. Gushers, as they are called, waste a lot of valuable petroleum. Modern wells are capped to keep this from happening.

✔ **How are petroleum and natural gas taken from the ground?**

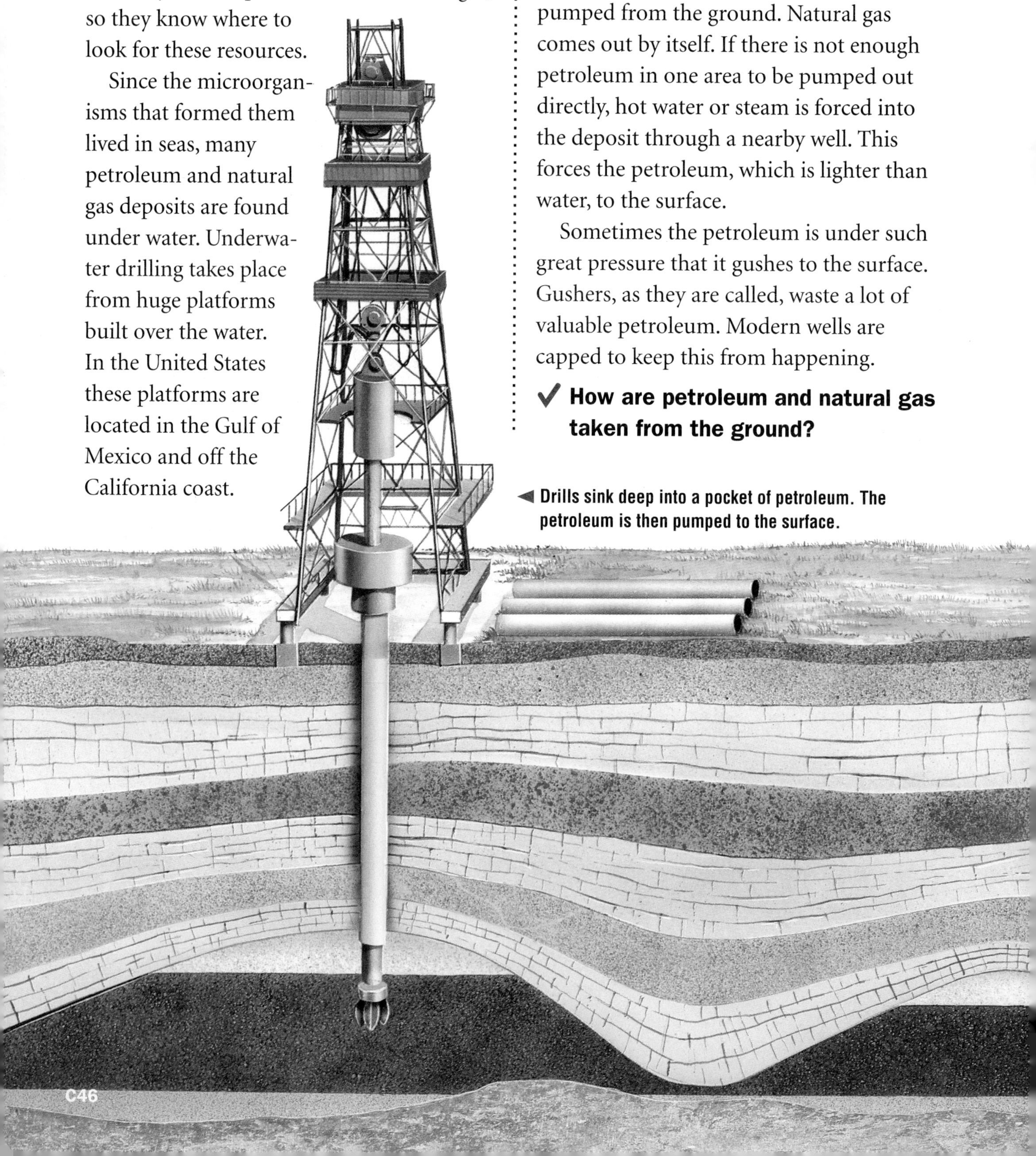

◀ **Drills sink deep into a pocket of petroleum. The petroleum is then pumped to the surface.**

Summary

Coal, oil, and natural gas are fossil fuels. Fossil fuels formed over millions of years from the decayed remains of organisms. Coal formation occurs in four stages, producing peat, lignite, bitumen, and anthracite. Petroleum and natural gas formed from microorganisms buried under ancient seas.

Review

1. List two products that contain petrochemicals made from petroleum.
2. What is most coal used for in the United States?
3. How did Earth's deposits of coal form?
4. **Critical Thinking** As coal forms, how does its carbon content change? How might this change affect its ability to heat?
5. **Test Prep** Which of these is **NOT** a stage in the formation of petroleum?
   - A Microorganisms sink to the bottom of shallow seas.
   - B Layers of mud pile on top of the remains.
   - C Organisms in mud produce new microorganisms.
   - D The remains slowly turn into petroleum.

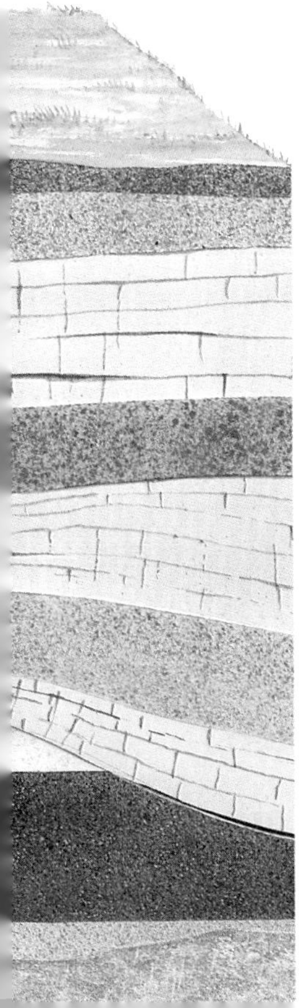

LINKS

MATH LINK

Petroleum Reserves Use a computer and a graphing program such as *Graph Links* to make a graph showing the world's top five producers of petroleum. How does the amount of petroleum the United States produces compare to that of other nations?

WRITING LINK

Informative Writing—Report As you watch TV commercials, look for those that show fossil fuels being used. Then write a commercial that shows ways fossil fuels could be conserved. Present your commercial to your class.

SOCIAL STUDIES LINK

History of Petroleum When was petroleum first discovered? How was it first used? Write a short report on the early history of petroleum.

TECHNOLOGY LINK

Learn more about the formation of fossil fuels by visiting this Internet site.
www.scilinks.org/harcourt

SCILINKS™ THE WORLD'S A CLICK AWAY

LESSON 3

How Are Natural Resources Conserved?

In this lesson, you can . . .

INVESTIGATE how people use natural resources.

LEARN ABOUT how people can conserve natural resources.

LINK to math, writing, social studies, and technology.

This Earth Day costume is made of old cans, paper, and bottles. ▼

INVESTIGATE

How People Use Natural Resources

Activity Purpose Suppose you're on a hike. You started out with three pieces of fruit and you have one piece left. You want to eat it, but you're not sure how long it will be before you can get more food. So you decide to save the fruit. You have reached an important conclusion—it is not always best to use everything right away, because the supply may run out. In this investigation you will **hypothesize** about how people can use resources without using them up too quickly.

Materials

- small bowl of paper clips
- 3 generation cards (parents, children, grandchildren)

Activity Procedure

1. Work in a group of three. Place your group's generation cards face down on a table. The bowl of paper clips stands for Earth's supply of a certain resource, such as iron.
2. Each person in the group now takes a generation card. Hold up your card so the other people in your group can see it. The card tells you your generation. It also tells you how many people are in your generation. (Picture A)

3. Each generation will now get paper clips from the bowl. The person from the parents' generation goes first. He or she takes five clips from the bowl for each person in his or her generation. (Picture B)

4. Next, the person from the children's generation takes five clips for each person in his or her generation.

5. Finally, the person from the grandchildren's generation takes five clips for each person in his or her generation.

Picture A

Picture B

Draw Conclusions

1. Did everyone get the same number of clips?
2. Where did a problem occur?
3. What could be done to avoid the problem?
4. **Scientists at Work** Scientists **hypothesize** what the results of an investigation might be. Hypothesize what will happen if each person from a generation gets only three or four clips, instead of five.

Investigate Further With the members of your group, list the products people use that are made from a natural resource, such as a certain metal. Describe several things people could do to make sure that in the future there will be enough of this resource. Then **plan and conduct a simple investigation** using technology to simulate your plan.

Process Skill Tip

When you **hypothesize,** you make a sensible guess about what might happen under certain conditions. You should base your hypothesis on observations, the results of previous experiments, or what you already know.

LEARN ABOUT

Conserving Natural Resources

FIND OUT

- why conserving natural resources is necessary
- how reusing and recycling can conserve resources

VOCABULARY

recycling

Making Choices

What would happen if one day there were no iron or petroleum or lumber? In the investigation you found out that using too much of a resource quickly can cause it to run out. The choices people make today about using natural resources can make the difference between having them in the future or not.

Earth's human population is growing, but the amounts of most natural resources are not. More people will demand more iron, oil, lumber, and other resources. Thinking about future demands for resources helps people plan ways to conserve them now. Conserving natural resources often involves choices. When you pour a glass of lemonade, do you use a disposable paper cup or a washable glass? Using a glass saves paper, but using a paper cup saves water.

Each decision has only a small effect on natural resources. But the choices of many people over time have a big effect. The photograph below shows land that was once a strip mine. The choices for this mined land were to leave it as it was after the coal was removed or to try to restore it to the way it had been before the coal was mined. Because people chose to restore the land, many will enjoy it in the future.

✓ What does conserving resources often involve?

The top layers of soil and rock were removed to mine coal. Soil, plants, and wildlife were destroyed. ▼

This mined land was partially restored by replacing the soil and planting grass and trees. Reclaimed land is a future resource.

▲ Instead of cutting down all the trees, people can do selective cutting, taking some trees and leaving others. The trees that are left help replace the cut trees by producing seeds.

◀ People can replant trees where they have been cut down.

Changing Behaviors

The simplest way to conserve natural resources is to use fewer resources. Using fewer aluminum cans, for example, means that less bauxite—aluminum ore—will have to be mined. Driving less or driving cars that are more fuel-efficient means that less petroleum will be needed. This works for nonrenewable resources. However, conserving renewable and reusable resources means saving them from damage and protecting them from overuse.

Saving resources from damage includes keeping them free of pollution. For many years, few people realized how dangerous pollution was to natural resources. Many people thought the supply of Earth's reusable resources was so large that nothing could damage it.

Now people realize that water pollution can kill fish and oxygen-producing microorganisms. People also know that air pollution can kill trees and make people sick. And garbage and rusting cars are just plain ugly. Most scientists agree that preventing pollution is an important part of conserving natural resources.

Renewable resources need protection from overuse. For example, in the early 1900s the hunting of whales was a big business. So many countries hunted whales that the population of blue whales, the largest whale species, was almost completely destroyed. In 1965 it became illegal to hunt blue whales in the Southern Hemisphere. This allowed the population to increase to the point that blue whales are now unlikely to become extinct. Today only Japan, Norway, and Russia hunt blue whales.

Forests are another renewable resource that needs protection from overuse. Forests are not just trees. They also provide habitats for many kinds of animals. Loss of habitat is the biggest threat to wildlife. Reasonable limits on the number of trees that can be cut allow forests to renew themselves. Selective cutting helps protect habitats for wildlife.

✔ **How can reusable and renewable resources be conserved?**

Reduce, Reuse, Recycle

People in the United States use more resources per person than most other people in the world. It takes 500,000 trees each week just to make the paper for Sunday newspapers. Every year, Americans throw away 28 billion glass bottles and jars. The average American uses about 90 kg (200 lb) of plastic each year—most of it in packaging that is thrown away.

One way to conserve resources is to reduce the amounts that are used. Using less energy conserves fossil fuels. Using less paper conserves forests. And using fewer bottles and cans conserves minerals.

Another way to conserve resources is to reuse things. Paper or plastic grocery bags can be reused by taking them back to the store, or they can be used as garbage bags or lunch bags.

Many things that can't be reused can be recycled. **Recycling** is the process of taking back a resource used to make a product. That resource is then made into a new product. Many communities have programs for collecting newspaper, glass, aluminum, and plastic. Trucks carry these materials to recycling centers where they are broken down into raw materials to make new products. In some states or communities, recycling is not just a good idea—it's the law.

Sometimes people choose disposable items because they are less expensive or easier to use. But if the materials can't be reused or recycled, the resources used in them will be lost. Recycling saves other resources, too. Recycling aluminum cans, for example, saves both minerals and fuel. The process of making new cans from recycled aluminum uses much less energy than making cans from bauxite does.

✔ **What is recycling?**

◀ The glass blower uses natural resources such as sand and limestone to make glass.

Long-life fluorescent light bulbs last longer, *reducing* the number of bulbs that have to be made. They use less energy, too. ▼

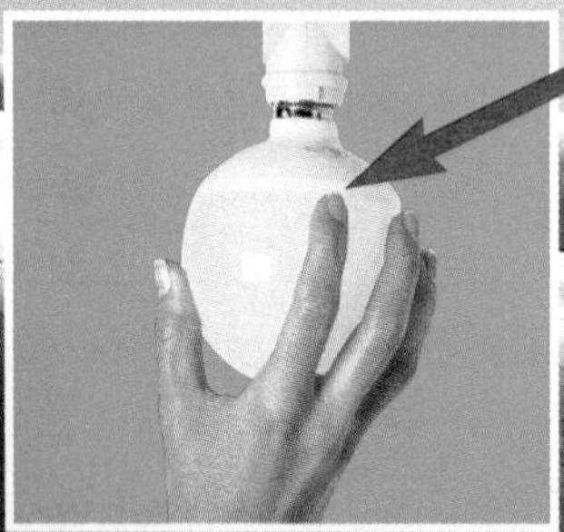

Glass bottles can be *recycled*. The glass is melted at high temperatures and formed into new products. ▼

A glass bottle can be *reused* for other things.

Although silica sand, used to make glass, seems to be inexhaustible, it is a nonrenewable resource.

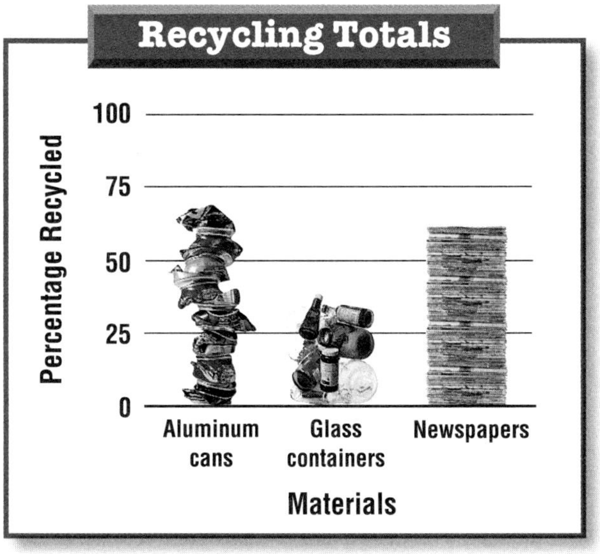

▲ Americans recycle almost 67 percent of their aluminum cans, 63 percent of their newspapers, and 38 percent of their glass containers.

Summary

Earth has a limited supply of natural resources. They must be conserved so that they will last as long as possible. Protecting resources from damage and overuse is a part of conservation. Reusing and recycling products saves resources needed to make new products.

Review

1. How does pollution harm natural resources?
2. What changes result from cutting down an old forest?
3. How does reusing products help conserve natural resources?
4. **Critical Thinking** How does using less electricity save natural resources?
5. **Test Prep** Which resource is **NOT** a type of natural resource?
   A reusable resource
   B renewable resource
   C remarkable resource
   D nonrenewable resource

LINKS

MATH LINK

Recycled Content Look for packaging that has *recycled* or *post-consumer content* on the label. Make a list of all the items you find, what each is made of, and how much of the material in each is recycled. Then make a circle graph for all the recycled packaging. The parts of the graph should show the percentages of recycled paper, plastic, aluminum, and glass in the packaging you find.

WRITING LINK

Informative Writing—How-To Make a poster for a school recycling program. Explain the recycling laws or policies in your community.

SOCIAL STUDIES LINK

Conservation Make a list of everything you used this morning. Did you use any recycled or reusable products? How did you conserve resources? How could you have conserved more? Share your ideas with a classmate.

TECHNOLOGY LINK

Learn more about conserving natural resources by visiting this Smithsonian Institution Internet site.
www.si.edu/harcourt/science

Smithsonian Institution®

Getting More Oil from Wells

Scientists and petroleum engineers are using water, gas, heat, and soap to help keep oil flowing from thousands of old oil wells.

Pumped Up

The petroleum, or oil, that people use is deposited in layers of rock. In some deposits, the oil forms large, flat pools between rock layers. In others it fills a network of tiny cracks within the rock. In still others, the oil is mixed with sand, the way sea water is mixed with sand at the beach.

If an oil deposit is deep below the surface, the weight of the rock above produces pressure on it. This makes it easy to get the oil out. Companies drill down to the deposit, and the oil rushes up to the surface. This pressure also keeps the oil flowing out of the well. When the pressure is too low to push the oil up through the well pipe, a pump can often pull it up. The use of this combination of natural pressure and pumping is known as primary oil production.

This photograph from the early 1900s shows an oil gusher in a California oil field. Gushers waste a lot of valuable oil.

Natural gas is burned off so the oil can be pumped from this offshore well.

However, primary production doesn't work on shallow deposits, and it won't get all the oil out of deep deposits. In fact, most deep wells are abandoned when only about one-third of the oil has been removed. Getting the rest of the oil out is too difficult or too expensive.

Wishing for Better Wells

Oil companies have usually looked for new places to drill for oil that is easy to recover. However, oil company geologists and engineers are now also working on ways to get the oil that primary production can't recover. The use of these new methods of getting more oil out of old wells is called secondary recovery or enhanced recovery.

One method used in secondary recovery is injection. Water or gas is pumped down into the ground near an oil well. This produces pressure that forces the oil into the well pipe. In some wells this method makes it possible to pump out about half the oil left after primary production. Injection can also be used to get oil from some shallow deposits.

Scientists at the U. S. Department of Energy are working on other secondary recovery methods, too. One, called thermal extraction, uses heat. Steam is pumped into the deposit. Heat from the steam makes the oil thinner, so it flows more easily. The steam also increases pressure.

Scientists are also mixing detergents with the water injected into wells. The soapy liquid makes the oil flow more easily. Other scientists are experimenting with microorganisms that "eat" oil. When these organisms digest some of the oil in a deposit, they produce gas (like millions of little burps!) that increases pressure in the well.

THINK ABOUT IT

1. What is a name for the use of methods of getting more oil out of old wells?
2. How does thermal extraction work?

WEB LINK:
For science and technology updates, visit The Learning Site.
www.harcourtschool.com

Careers Oil Rig Worker

What They Do Oil rig workers help drill new wells and help keep old wells productive.

Education and Training Most oil rig workers train on the job. They start by handling pipe and learn to work with complicated drilling machinery.

PEOPLE IN SCIENCE

Paul D. MacCready

ENGINEER

"If you have the enthusiasm to charge ahead, you can do all sorts of things. People can do so much more than they realize."

Paul MacCready is best known as the inventor of the *Gossamer Condor,* the world's first successful human-powered flying machine. Yet this remarkable invention is only one of many accomplishments of this creative engineer. Dr. MacCready has won the U.S. soaring championship four times in his gliders, which are aircraft without engines. He was also the first American to win the world soaring championship. His second human-powered vehicle, the *Gossamer Albatross,* was the first human-powered aircraft to cross the English Channel. A third invention, the *Bionic Bat,* set a record for human-powered speed.

Dr. MacCready has done more than invent human-powered aircraft. He has also worked to develop environmentally friendly forms of transportation. In 1987 he built a solar-powered car, the Sunraycer, which competed in a race across Australia. In 1990 he worked with General Motors to develop the Impact, an electric car.

Today Dr. MacCready is working for AeroVironment, a company he founded in 1971 in Monrovia, California. He and his partners help businesses learn about environmental issues and wind power. They also design remote-controlled electric airplanes, which are used by the Department of Defense to gather information.

THINK ABOUT IT

1. How has Dr. MacCready combined his interests in soaring, engineering, and business?
2. How might the use of Dr. MacCready's vehicles help the environment?

The *Centurion,* an atmospheric research aircraft

Minerals

How can you identify minerals from their crystals?

Materials

- talcum powder
- table salt
- chalk
- black construction paper
- hand lens
- microscope slides
- microscope

Procedure

1. Put a little talcum powder, chalk, and table salt on a sheet of black construction paper. Observe each substance with the hand lens.

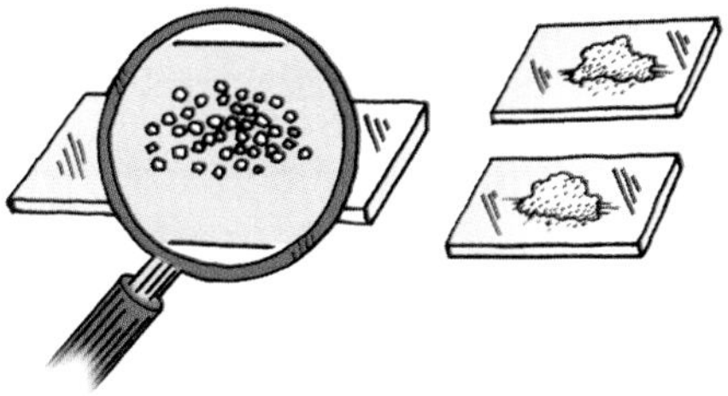

2. Put a little of each substance on a microscope slide. Observe under low power of the microscope.
3. Now mix the three substances together on a microscope slide. Observe the mixture under low power.
4. Try to identify each substance in the mixture.

Draw Conclusions

Talc, salt, and chalk are all minerals. Some minerals form crystals with regular shapes. What shape are the salt crystals? How are the talc and chalk different from the salt? How could you separate a mixture of the three minerals?

The 3 *R*s

What objects could be reduced, reused, or recycled?

Materials

- paper
- pencil

Procedure

1. Fold the paper into three columns.
2. Label the columns "Reduce," "Reuse," and "Recycle."

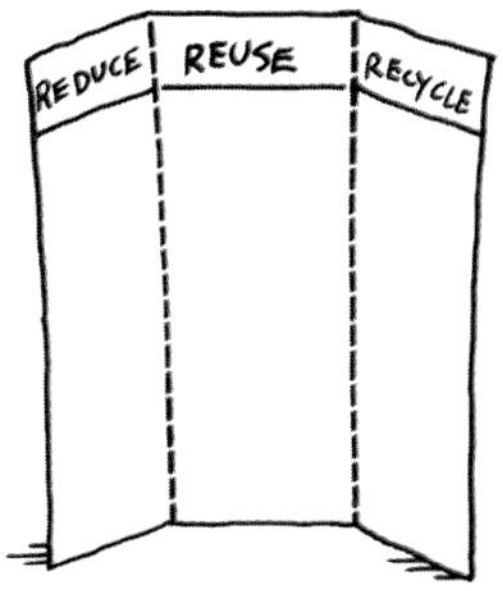

3. As you go through your day at school, write in the appropriate column each object you use that could be reduced in amount, reused in another way, or recycled to make a new object.

Draw Conclusions

How many objects did you list in each column? Compare your lists with those of your classmates. Then every day for a week, choose an object from one column and for that day, reduce the amount you use, reuse the object in a different way, or recycle the object.

Chapter 2 Review and Test Preparation

Vocabulary Review

Use the terms below to complete the sentences. The page numbers in ( ) tell you where to look in the chapter if you need help.

natural resource (C36)
nonrenewable resource (C36)
fossil fuel (C42)
renewable resource (C38)
reusable resource (C38)
natural gas (C43)
peat (C44)
lignite (C44)
bitumen (C45)
anthracite (C45)
recycling (C52)

1. A ____ is a resource that can be replaced as it is used.

2. A hard, black form of coal is ____.

3. A soft, brown material made up of partly decayed plants is ____.

4. ____ is the process of taking a resource back from a product.

5. A ____ is a useful mineral or other material that people take from the Earth.

6. ____ is a gas made up mostly of methane.

7. A soft, brown form of coal is ____.

8. A ____ is a resource that cannot be replaced once it is used.

9. A ____ is a resource that can be used more than once.

10. ____ is a fairly hard, dark brown or black form of coal.

11. A ____ is a fuel such as coal, petroleum, and natural gas that formed in the Earth from decayed organisms.

Connect Concepts

Use the Word Bank to complete the chart. List the three main categories of natural resources on the top lines. Then list an example of each type of resource on the lines below.

minerals/rocks	**soil**	**forests**
nonrenewable	**coal**	**fossil**
renewable	**water**	**reusable**
natural gas	**air**	**petroleum**

Three Categories of Natural Resources

12. ________	**19.** ____	**21.** ____
13. ________		22. ____
14. ____ fuels		
Three types of the resource in #14:	20. ____	23. ____
15. ________		
16. ________		
17. ________		
18. ________		

Check Understanding

Write the letter of the best choice.

24. All natural resources are —
- **A** useful materials that can be replaced
- **B** useful materials that cannot be replaced
- **C** useful materials that are used for fuel
- **D** useful materials that people take from the Earth

25. Fossil fuels are important to us because —
   - **F** they produce heat when burned
   - **G** they are reusable resources
   - **H** they are the only fuels used to make electricity
   - **J** they are renewable resources

26. Conservation of natural resources could include —
   - **A** the use of more renewable sources of energy
   - **B** cutting down on the use of fossil fuels
   - **C** replacing soil and planting trees
   - **D** all of the above

27. Fossil fuels include —
   - **F** jet fuel, graphite, and lead
   - **G** bauxite, oil, and coal
   - **H** natural gas, oil, and coal
   - **J** coal, oil, and peat

28. The stages of coal formation, in order, are —
   - **A** peat, lignite, bitumen, anthracite
   - **B** bitumen, anthracite, peat, lignite
   - **C** anthracite, peat, lignite, bitumen
   - **D** lignite, bitumen, anthracite, peat

Critical Thinking

29. How would your life be different if water were a nonrenewable resource?

30. Most electricity is produced using fossil fuels. Some people think electricity should be produced using resources such as wind, water, and solar energy. Why might people have this opinion?

31. How does recycling plastic conserve fossil fuels?

Process Skills Review

32. **Predict** what might happen to nonrenewable resources as the population increases.

33. Assume that the recycling rate for aluminum cans is 66 percent and that the recycling rate for all other aluminum is 38 percent. **Use numbers** to **infer** the recycling rate of aluminum foil and building materials.

34. Wildlife is a renewable resource. **Predict** what would happen if the number of animals born to a species were less than the number killed by hunters. How could conservation change this?

Performance Assessment

Identifying Resources

Classify the resources needed for each of the following objects or activities as *nonrenewable, renewable, or reusable:* a cotton T-shirt; water used to bathe; a ride on a school bus; a pencil; this book; a glass bottle; and electricity produced by wind energy.

Chapter 3

Weather and Climate

Does weather begin or end? Or does it just keep moving from place to place? Many things contribute to making weather and to changing it.

Vocabulary Preview

- atmosphere
- air pressure
- humidity
- precipitation
- evaporation
- condensation
- local winds
- prevailing winds
- climate
- microclimate
- El Niño
- greenhouse effect
- global warming

FAST FACT

The United States is a country of many weather extremes. Below are some record-breaking weather measurements.

Heavy Weather

What	Where	How Much
Highest Temperature	Death Valley, CA	134°F
Lowest Temperature	Prospect Creek, AK	−79.8°F
Heaviest Snowfall	Mount Shasta, CA	189 in.
Most Snow in a Year	Mount Rainier, WA	1,224.5 in.
Strongest Wind	Mount Washington, NH	231 mi/hr
Most Rain in a Year	Kukui, HI	739 in.

FAST FACT

Each summer an average of 6–12 tropical storms form in the Atlantic Ocean, the Caribbean Sea, or the Gulf of Mexico and move toward the United States. If a storm's winds reach 74 miles an hour or more, the storm is called a hurricane.

FAST FACT

In 1816 a volcano in Asia blew huge amounts of dust into the atmosphere, blocking some of the sun's rays. That year average temperatures around the world dropped several degrees. In June there were even a few days of snow in the northeastern United States.

LESSON 1

How Can You Observe and Measure Weather Conditions?

In this lesson, you can . . .

INVESTIGATE and measure weather conditions.

LEARN ABOUT Earth's weather systems.

LINK to math, writing, art, and technology.

INVESTIGATE

Measuring Weather Conditions

Activity Purpose

People have always been affected by the weather. But it wasn't until fairly recently that scientists have been able to predict the weather accurately. Today's weather scientists use many instruments to **measure** and **collect data** about weather conditions. Then they use the data to help **predict** what the weather will be like today, tomorrow, or next weekend. In this investigation you will measure and collect data about weather conditions in your area.

Materials

- weather station

Activity Procedure

1. Make a copy of the Weather Station Daily Record table. You will use it to **record** the date, the time, the temperature, the amount of rain or snow, the wind direction and speed, and the cloud conditions each day for five days. Try to **record** the weather conditions at the same time each day.
2. Place the weather station in a shady spot, 1 m above the ground. **Record** the temperature. (Picture A)
3. Be sure the rain gauge will not collect runoff from any buildings or trees. **Record** the amount of rain or snow (if any).

◄ A Midwest tornado

Weather Station Daily Record

Date					
Time					
Temperature					
Rainfall or snowfall					
Wind direction and speed					
Cloud conditions					

Picture A

4. Be sure the wind vane is located where wind from any direction will reach it. **Record** the wind direction and speed. Winds are labeled with the direction from which they blow. (Picture B)

5. Describe and **record** the cloud conditions by noting how much of the sky is covered by clouds. Draw a circle and shade in the part of the circle that equals the amount of sky covered with clouds.

6. Use the temperature data to make a line graph showing how the temperature changes from day to day.

Picture B

Draw Conclusions

1. Use your Weather Station Daily Record to **compare** the weather conditions on two different days. Which conditions were about the same? Which conditions changed the most?
2. From the **data** you **gathered** in this activity, how might scientists use weather data to **predict** the weather?
3. **Scientists at Work** Scientists learn about the weather by **measuring** weather conditions and **gathering data.** What did you learn by measuring the amount of rain your area received during the week of your observations?

Investigate Further Find a newspaper weather page, and note the temperatures in various cities throughout the United States. Why are there different temperatures in different cities? **Plan and conduct a simple investigation** using technology to find out.

Process Skill Tip

Measurements are a kind of observation. You **measure** when you use a tool, such as a thermometer or rain gauge, to **gather data** about something.

LEARN ABOUT

Weather Systems

FIND OUT

- where most weather occurs
- how weather conditions are measured
- how clouds form

VOCABULARY

atmosphere
air pressure
humidity
precipitation
evaporation
condensation

Where Weather Occurs

Almost all weather occurs in the lowest layer of air, or **atmosphere**, that surrounds Earth. The atmosphere stretches about 1000 km (620 mi) from the Earth's surface to outer space. The lowest layer of the atmosphere, called the *troposphere*, is where most water is found and where most clouds form. The troposphere is about 15 km (9 mi) thick at the equator.

Very little weather occurs above the troposphere. There is a little water in the *stratosphere,* the next higher layer, so a few clouds form there. But more important is the stratosphere's ozone layer, about 22.5 km (14 mi) above the Earth's surface. Ozone protects life on Earth by absorbing some of the sun's harmful rays. From the stratosphere to the edge of space, there is no water and too little air for any weather to occur.

✓ **In what layer of the atmosphere does most of Earth's weather occur?**

Blizzards, at the left, and hurricanes at the right, are among the largest and most powerful weather systems of Earth's troposphere, shown below.

A *thermometer* measures air temperature. ▼

Air pressure is the weight of the atmosphere. A *barometer* measures air pressure. ▼

A *rain gauge* measures the amount of precipitation. ▼

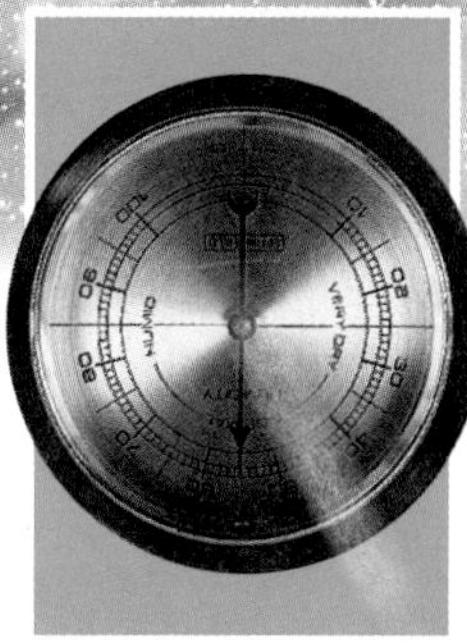

◀ Water in the air is called humidity. A *hygrometer* (hy•GRAHM•uht•er) measures humidity.

A *wind vane* measures the direction from which the wind is blowing. An *anemometer* (an•uh•MAHM•uht•er) measures wind speed. ▶

Measuring Atmospheric Conditions

The weather changes because the atmosphere is constantly changing. Sometimes the air is cold and sometimes it's warm. As air warms, its weight, or **air pressure**, lessens. And warm air holds more water, or can have more **humidity**, than cold air. These and other conditions of the atmosphere can be observed and measured.

The weather instruments shown on this page can be used to measure atmospheric conditions—air temperature, air pressure, **precipitation** (rain or snow), humidity, wind direction, and wind speed. Other atmospheric conditions, such as cloud type, are observed directly.

Why do people measure atmospheric conditions? One reason is to predict what the weather will be. For example, a change in air pressure or cloud type often means there will be a change in the weather.

✔ **What are some atmospheric conditions that can be measured?**

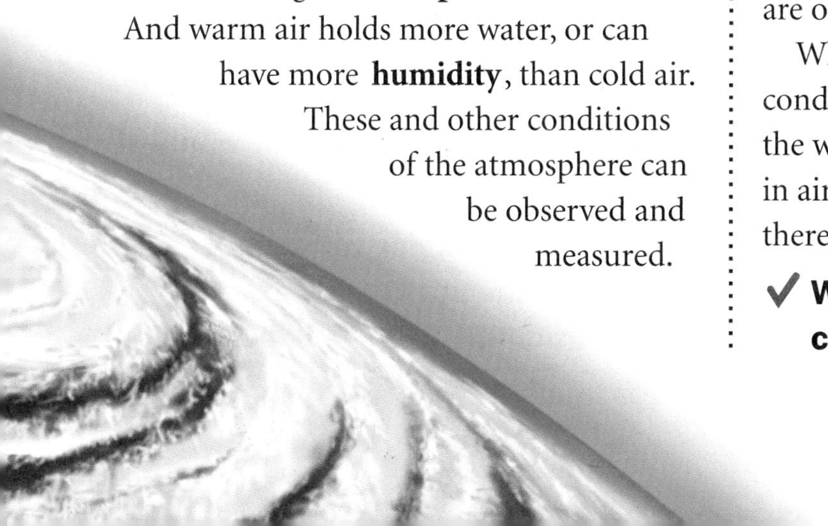

Air Pressure

You probably don't feel the atmosphere weighing you down. But air does have weight. The atmosphere pushes on you all the time, and this weight is air pressure.

There are several types of barometers for measuring air pressure. A mercury barometer, like the ones shown at the right, consists of a glass tube about 1 m (3 ft) long. Air is removed from the tube, and the glass is sealed at the top. Then the tube is turned upside down, and the open end is placed in a dish of mercury. The weight of the air pushing down on the mercury in the dish pushes mercury up into the glass tube. The mercury rises in the tube until its weight exactly balances the weight of the air pushing down on the mercury in the dish. The height of the mercury in the tube is a measure of air pressure. This measure is compared to a standard, or average, air pressure of about 76 cm (30 in.) of mercury.

Recall that warm air weighs less than cold air. A mass of cold air, called a *high-pressure area,* will measure more than 76 cm of mercury. A mass of warm air, called a *low-pressure area,* will measure less than 76 cm of mercury.

Weather changes because high- and low-pressure areas move. In the winter, areas of high pressure often move from northwestern Canada toward the southeastern United States, bringing cool, dry weather conditions. In the summer, areas of low pressure often move from the Gulf of Mexico to the northeastern United States, bringing warm, wet weather conditions.

As these high-pressure and low-pressure areas move, barometer readings in their paths change. Therefore, changing barometer readings can be used to predict changes in weather. If the barometer is rising, the weather will probably become fair. If the barometer is falling, stormy weather is probably coming.

HIGH AIR PRESSURE

The mercury in this barometer is high. Areas of high pressure usually have fair weather.

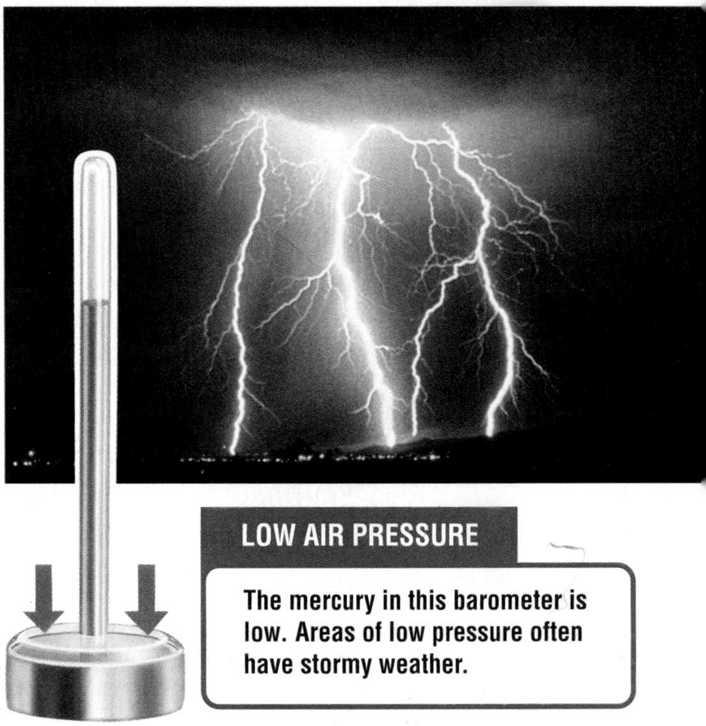

LOW AIR PRESSURE

The mercury in this barometer is low. Areas of low pressure often have stormy weather.

✔ **How can changing air pressure be used to predict changing weather conditions?**

Water in the Air

In addition to temperature and air pressure, humidity, or the amount of water in the air, is an important factor in describing weather conditions. But how does water get into the air?

Earth's oceans are the biggest source of water. As the sun heats the oceans, liquid water changes into an invisible gas called *water vapor,* which rises into the air. The process of liquid water changing to water vapor is called **evaporation**. High up in the atmosphere, where the air is cooler, water vapor turns back into liquid drops of water, forming clouds. This process is called **condensation**.

When cloud drops come together, gravity returns the water to the Earth's surface as precipitation—usually rain. If the temperature in the clouds is below freezing, the precipitation is sleet, hail, or snow. This transferring of water from the Earth's surface to the atmosphere and back is called the *water cycle.*

THE INSIDE STORY

The Water Cycle

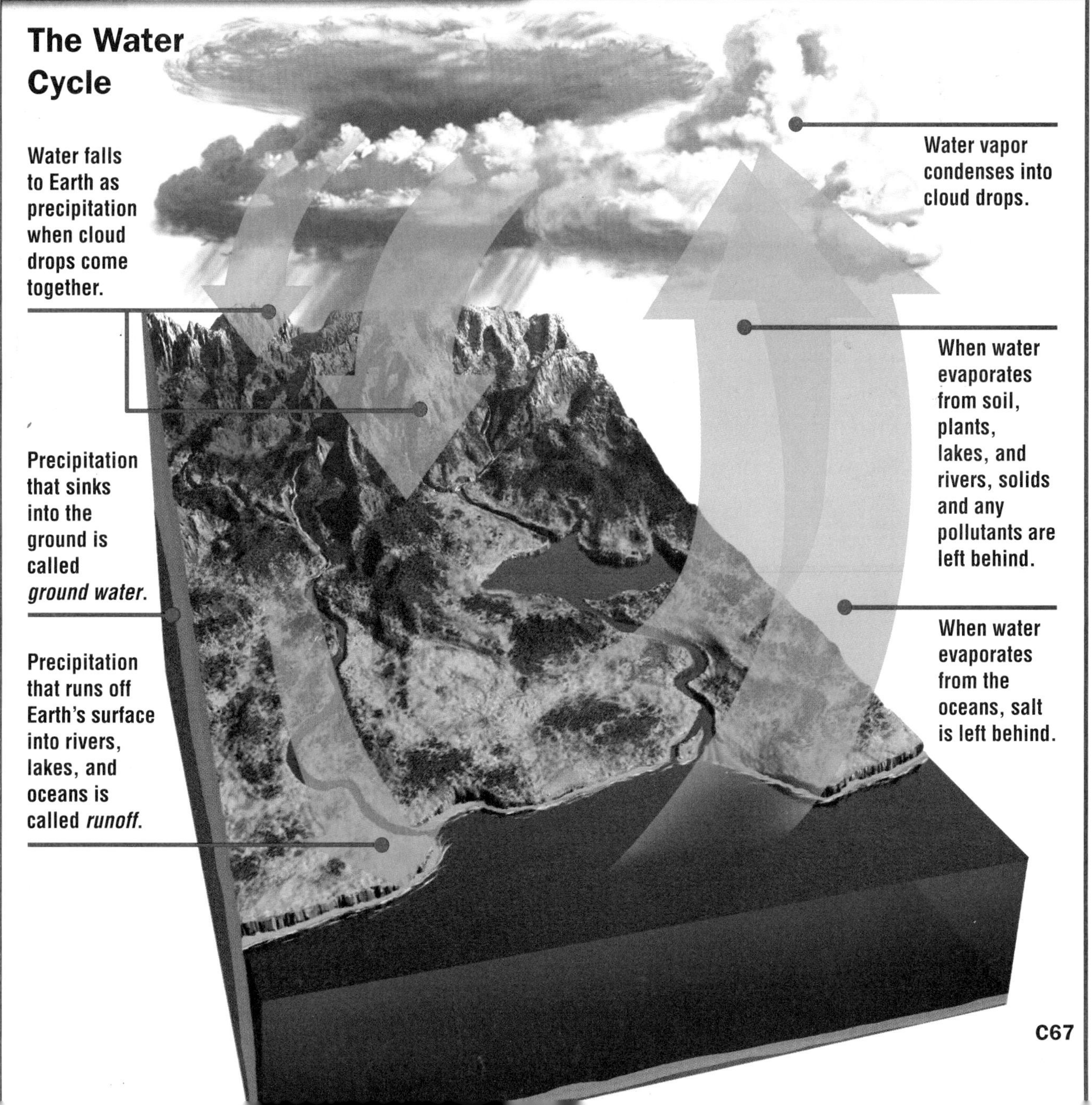

On clear nights, when the surface of the Earth cools quickly, water vapor may condense to form a cloud near the ground. This low cloud is called *fog*. If you have ever walked through fog, you know what the inside of a cloud is like.

Whether a cloud forms near the ground or high in the atmosphere, it forms in the same way. Water vapor condenses onto dust and other tiny particles in the air when it rises and cools. Another way in which air cools enough for water vapor to condense is by moving from a warm place to a colder place. For example, moist air that moves from over a warm body of water to over cooler land forms clouds or fog.

Even though all clouds form by condensation, different weather conditions produce different types of clouds. Weather scientists, or *meteorologists* (meet•ee•uhr•AHL•uh•juhsts),

Types of Clouds

▲ ***Cumulonimbus*** **(kyoo•myoo•loh•NIM•buhs) clouds are a type of cumulus cloud. Cumulonimbus clouds are tall and bring thundershowers and sometimes hail. These clouds are also called thunderheads or thunderclouds.**

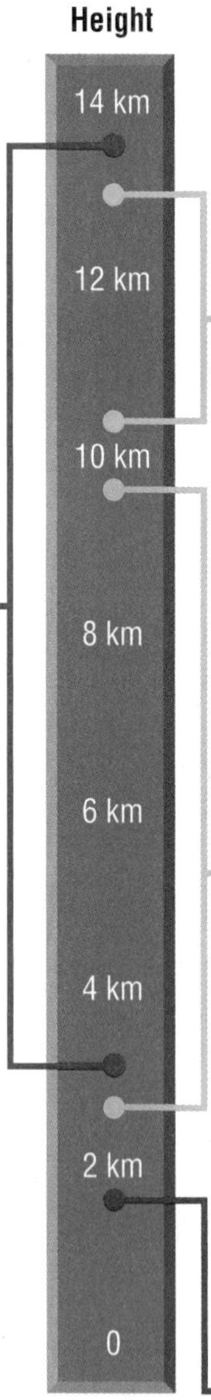

Cirrus **clouds are high clouds made mostly of ice crystals. They look thin and wispy. *Cirrus* means "curl of hair." Cirrus clouds are usually associated with fair weather, but they may mean that a change in weather conditions is coming. ►**

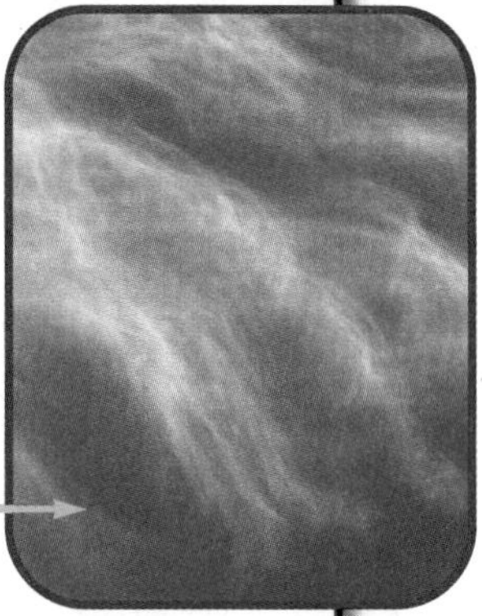

Cumulus **clouds form when large bubbles of warm air rise rapidly into the atmosphere. They look piled up and puffy. *Cumulus* means "heap." Cumulus clouds usually mean fair weather, but they can produce light rain or snow showers. ►**

Stratus **clouds form as a mass of warm air is slowly pushed upward over a mass of colder air or over a mountain. *Stratus* means "layer," and these clouds form layers. Stratus clouds near the ground are called *fog*. Stratus clouds often produce rain or snow. ►**

give clouds three basic names—cirrus (SEER•uhs), cumulus (KYOO•myoo•luhs), and stratus. Along with other information, the types of clouds in the atmosphere can be used to help predict weather changes. Some basic types of clouds and their descriptions are shown on page C68.

✓ **How do clouds form?**

Summary

Most of Earth's weather takes place in the troposphere, the lowest layer of the atmosphere. Weather conditions such as temperature, air pressure, humidity, wind speed and direction, and the amount of precipitation can be observed and measured. Certain weather conditions, such as changing air pressure and types of clouds, can be used to predict changes in the weather.

Review

1. How do weather scientists **observe** and **measure** weather conditions?
2. How is water recycled in the water cycle?
3. What causes clouds to form?
4. **Critical Thinking** It is a gray, cloudy day, and a light rain is falling. What type of clouds would you expect to see? Explain your answer.
5. **Test Prep** The process by which water vapor turns into liquid water drops is known as —
   A condensation
   B evaporation
   C precipitation
   D the water cycle

LINKS

MATH LINK

Measurement Many meteorologists in the United States measure air pressure in units called *millibars*. At sea level, standard air pressure is 1013.2 millibars. If 1013.2 millibars equals 76 cm of mercury, what would a barometer reading of 75 cm of mercury equal in millibars?

WRITING LINK

Informative Writing—Report Suppose that you are a meteorologist who has just spotted a large cumulonimbus cloud moving toward a city. Write a weather report for the city's residents.

ART LINK

Stormy Weather Make a drawing that includes one or more of the cloud types shown on page C68. Show the weather conditions that are associated with those cloud types.

TECHNOLOGY LINK

Learn more about Earth's atmosphere by visiting the Harcourt Learning Site.
www.harcourtschool.com

WELCOME TO THE LEARNING SITE

LESSON 2

What Causes Wind?

In this lesson, you can . . .

INVESTIGATE the rates at which water and soil absorb and release heat.

LEARN ABOUT uneven heating of the Earth's surface as the cause of wind.

LINK to math, writing, music, and technology.

INVESTIGATE

The Sun's Energy Heats Unevenly

Activity Purpose If you've ever walked barefoot from pavement to grass on a sunny day, you know that different materials absorb heat differently. On a larger scale, uneven heating like this is what produces wind. In this investigation you will **predict** which material heats up and cools off faster—water or soil. Then you will test your predictions.

Materials

- 2 tin cans (lids removed)
- water
- dry soil
- spoon
- 2 thermometers

Activity Procedure

1. Fill one can about $\frac{3}{4}$ full of water and the other can about $\frac{3}{4}$ full of soil. (Picture A)
2. Place one thermometer in the can of water and the other in the can of soil. Put the cans in a shady place outside. Wait for 10 minutes, and then **record** the temperatures of the water and the soil.
3. Put both cans in sunlight. **Predict** which of the cans will show the faster rise in temperature. **Record** the temperature of each can every 10 minutes for 30 minutes. In which can does the temperature rise faster? Which material—soil or water—heats up faster? (Picture B)

◀ Energy to fly this kite starts with the sun.

Picture A

Picture B

4. Now put the cans back in the shade. **Predict** in which of the cans the temperature will drop faster. Again **record** the temperature of each can every 10 minutes for 30 minutes. In which can does the temperature drop faster? Which material—soil or water—cools off faster?

5. Make line graphs to show how the temperatures of both materials changed as they heated up and cooled off.

Draw Conclusions

1. How did your results match your predictions? Which material—water or soil—heated up faster? Which cooled off faster?
2. From the results you **observed** in this investigation, which would you **predict** heats up faster—oceans or land? Which would you predict cools off faster? Explain.
3. **Scientists at Work** Scientists learn by **predicting** and then testing their predictions. How did you test your predictions about water and soil?

Investigate Further **Predict** how fast other materials, such as moist soil, sand, and salt water, heat up and cool off. **Plan and conduct a simple investigation** to test your predictions.

Process Skill Tip

A prediction is based on previous observations. Before you **predict**, think about what you have already observed.

LEARN ABOUT

The Causes of Wind

FIND OUT

- what causes the wind
- about Earth's wind patterns

VOCABULARY

local winds

prevailing winds

Uneven Heating

The illustration below shows how the sun's rays strike the Earth's surface and the atmosphere. The atmosphere absorbs some of the sun's energy and reflects some of it back into space. Some of the energy that reaches the Earth's surface is reflected back into the atmosphere. However, much of the sun's energy is absorbed by the Earth's surface.

In the investigation you discovered that soil heats up faster and cools off faster than water. In the same way, when the sun's rays strike the Earth's surface, land absorbs the sun's energy more quickly and heats up faster than bodies of water, such as lakes, rivers, and oceans. And land releases heat and cools off faster when the sun goes down than bodies of water do.

✓ **What happens to the energy from the sun's rays that reach Earth?**

The atmosphere absorbs energy directly from the sun and from energy reflected from the Earth's surface. ▼

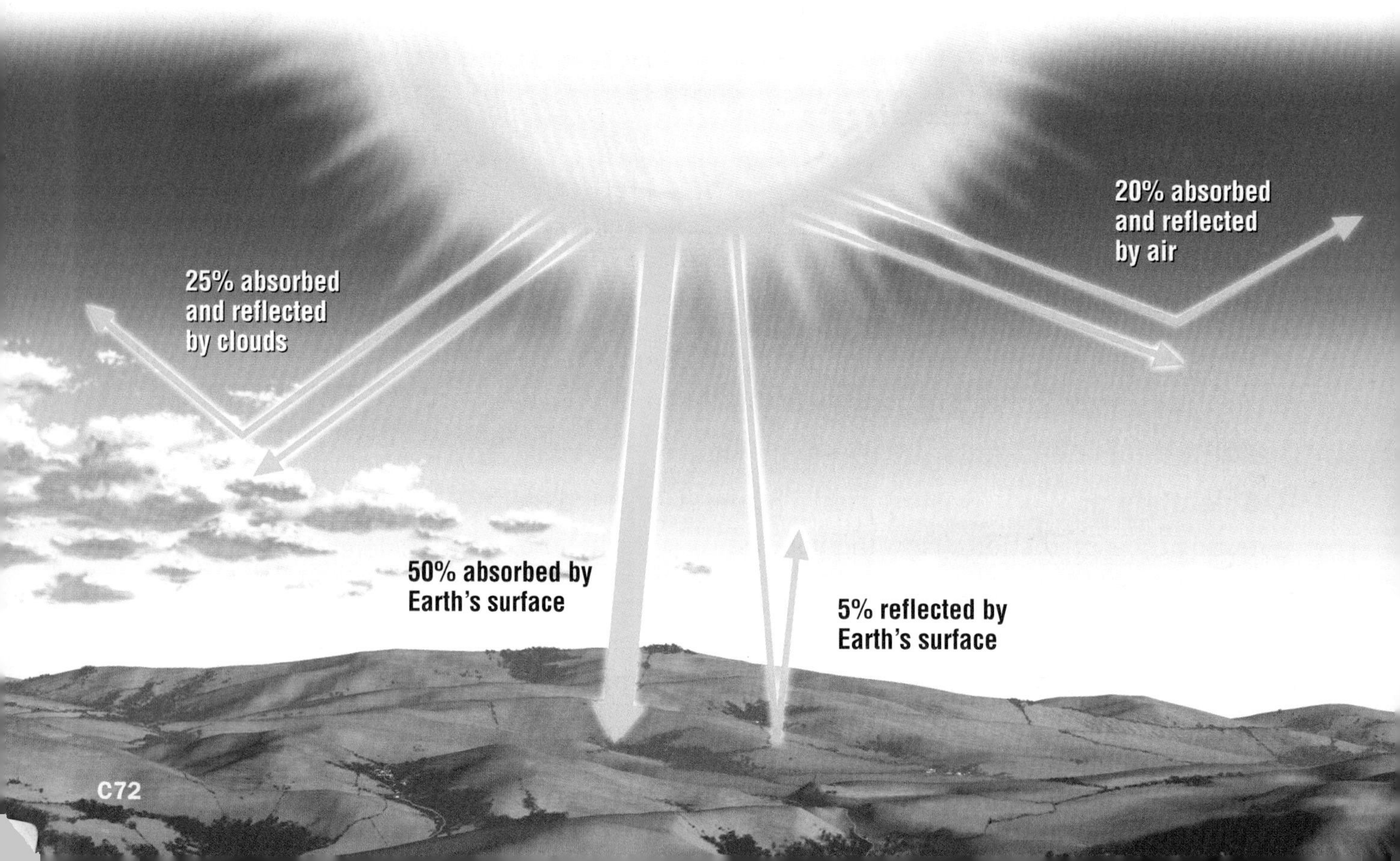

Local Winds

Because the Earth's surface is heated unevenly, the air above it is in constant motion. Cold air is heavier than warm air, so it sinks, forcing lighter, warm air to rise. The upward movement of warm air in the atmosphere produces *updrafts*. You may have seen birds soaring on updrafts.

At the surface, two places can often have differences in temperature and, therefore, differences in air pressure. These differences cause air to move from the area of higher pressure to the area of lower pressure. This horizontal movement of air is called *wind*. Winds can be local, affecting small areas, or global, affecting large parts of the Earth.

Local winds depend on local changes in temperature. The illustrations below show an example of local winds at the seashore. During the day, the land heats up more quickly than the water does, so the breezes blow from the sea to the land. But at night, air over the water is warmer than air over the land, so the breezes blow from the land to the sea.

✔ **What causes local winds?**

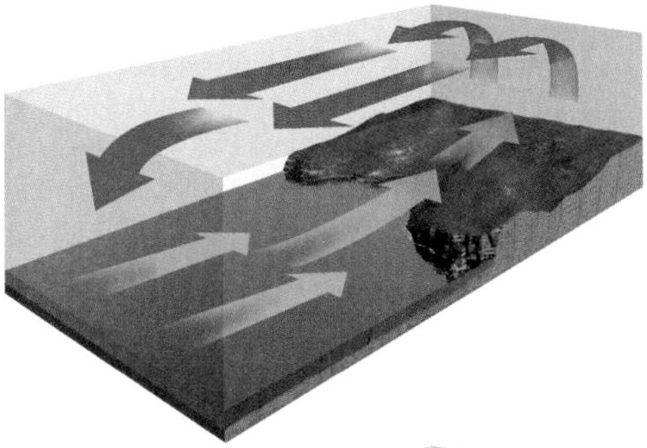

◀ During the day, the land heats up faster than the sea. Cooler sea air moves toward the land. This is called a sea breeze.

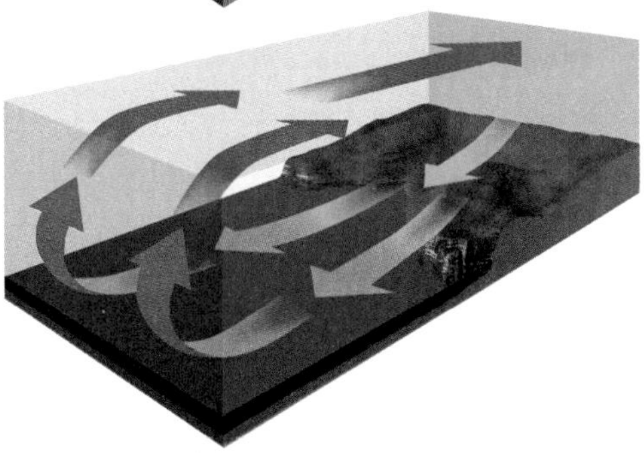

◀ At night, the land loses heat faster than the sea. Cooler air over the land moves toward the sea. This is called a land breeze.

▲ Uneven heating of the Earth's surface produces air masses of different temperatures. Cold air sinks, forcing warm air to rise.

Prevailing Winds

In the age of sailing ships, sailors relied on prevailing winds to carry them across the oceans. **Prevailing winds** are global winds that blow constantly from the same direction. Prevailing winds are caused by the uneven heating of large parts of Earth's atmosphere and by Earth's rotation.

To understand prevailing winds, first suppose an Earth that doesn't rotate. The sun warms the air over the equator, while air over the North and South Poles is very cold. The cold, heavy polar air flows toward the equator, forcing an upward movement of the warmed air at the equator. This air then flows north and south toward the poles. Far from the equator, the warm air cools and sinks at the poles, where it once again flows toward the equator. This flow from the equator to the poles and then back again is continuous.

Global Winds

The global winds that blow over most of the United States are the prevailing westerlies.

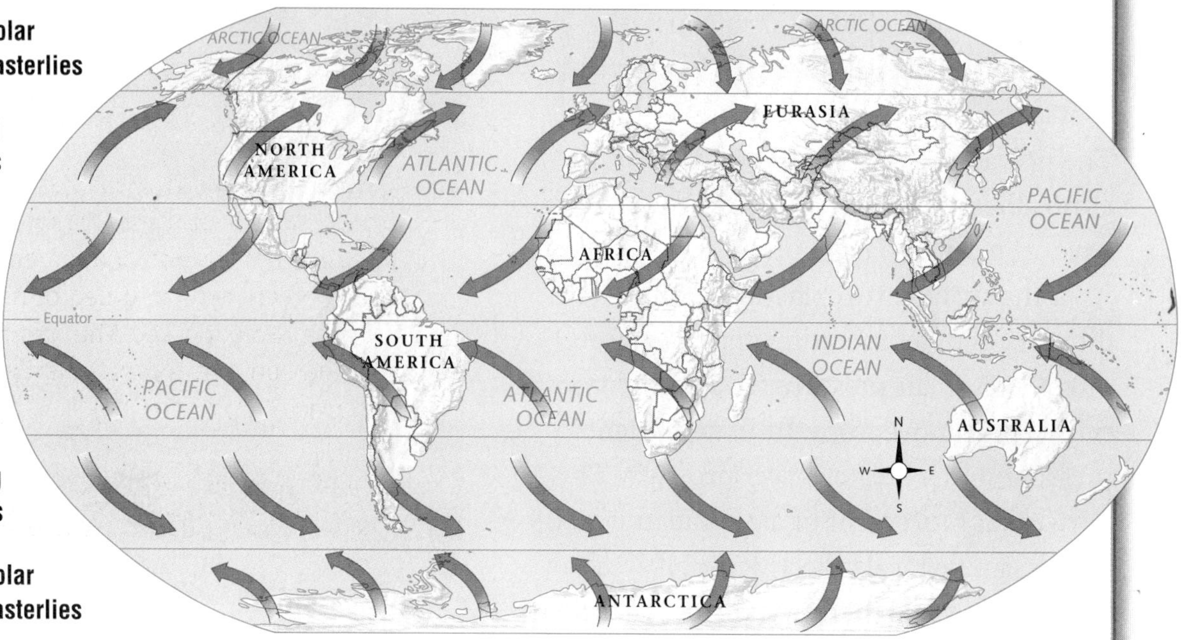

Now suppose Earth rotating from west to east. This rotation makes north and south winds curve. You can see this by placing a sheet of paper on a turntable. As the paper spins, try drawing a straight line from the center of the turntable to its edge.

Winds that blow toward the poles curve east. Winds that blow toward the equator curve west. In most of the United States, the prevailing winds curve to the east, producing west winds, or *westerlies.*

The prevailing westerlies cause most weather systems in the United States to move from west to east. Weather conditions on the West Coast today often move to the middle of the country tomorrow and from there to the East Coast the next day.

Weather Map

Weather in the United States usually moves from the west to the east. What kind of weather do you think Atlanta will have in the next day or so? Explain. ▶

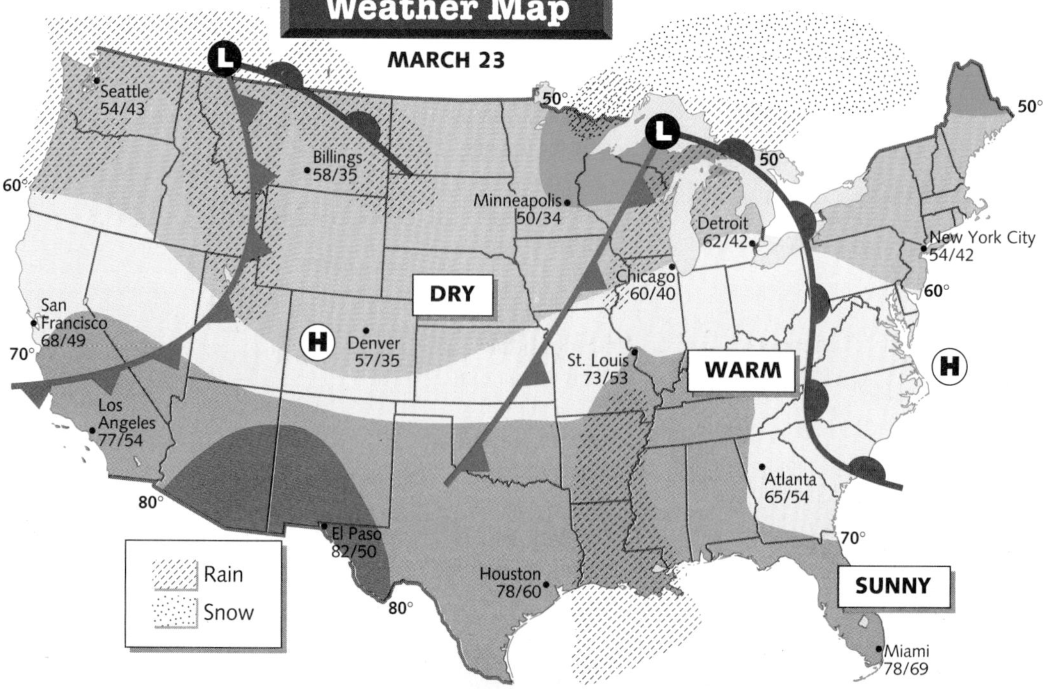

Look at the weather map at the bottom of page C74. Weather forecasters use maps to show how weather systems move. Forecasters also use maps to help predict weather changes.

✔ **What causes weather systems to move from west to east?**

Summary

Changes in air pressure, from uneven heating of Earth's surface and the air above it, cause the wind to blow. Local winds depend on local changes in temperature. Prevailing, or global, winds are caused by the sun's uneven heating of large parts of the atmosphere and by Earth's rotation on its axis. Prevailing winds in the United States are from the west, so weather systems tend to move from west to east.

Review

1. How does uneven heating of Earth's surface produce wind?
2. Suppose you're at the seashore on a sunny summer day. In which direction is the wind blowing? Why?
3. How do the prevailing winds affect weather systems in the United States?
4. **Critical Thinking** Shortly after daybreak at the seashore, the air temperature over sea and land is about the same. What sort of wind, if any, is blowing? Explain.
5. **Test Prep** A weather map can be used to show —
   A precipitation only
   B how and where weather systems move
   C local winds
   D prevailing winds

LINKS

MATH LINK

Calculate About 35 percent of the sun's rays that reach the Earth are reflected back into space. Another 15 percent are absorbed or reflected by the atmosphere. What percentage of the sun's rays reach the Earth's surface?

WRITING LINK

Expressive Writing—Friendly Letter Suppose you are on vacation. Write a postcard describing the weather to a friend. Include temperature, wind speed, and wind direction.

MUSIC LINK

Weather Songs Many songs are about the weather or compare something to the weather. Some examples are "You Are My Sunshine," "The Itsy Bitsy Spider," and "Sunny Day." Work with a partner to see how many weather songs you can list.

TECHNOLOGY LINK

Learn more about weather conditions and predictions by investigating *Umbrella or Not?* on the **Harcourt Science Explorations CD-ROM.**

LESSON 3

What Is Climate and How Does It Change?

In this lesson, you can . . .

INVESTIGATE local weather conditions.

LEARN ABOUT climates and how they change.

LINK to math, writing, literature, and technology.

INVESTIGATE

Local Weather Conditions

Activity Purpose Why does the temperature change as you go from the city to the country? Why is a city park cooler than nearby streets and sidewalks? You know that different parts of the country often have different weather conditions. In this investigation you'll find out if places very close to each other can have different weather conditions, too.

Materials

- 4 metersticks
- 4 weather stations

Activity Procedure

1. Make a table like the one shown on page C77.
2. Choose four locations near your school to study. Select different kinds of locations, such as a shady parkway, a sunny playground, a parking lot on the south side of your school, and a ball field on the north side. For the same time on any given day, **predict** whether the temperature, wind direction, and wind speed will be the same or different at the different locations.
3. At the chosen time, four people should each take a meterstick and a weather station to a different one of the selected locations. Use the meterstick to locate a point 1 m above the ground. **Measure** and **record** the temperature at that point. Use the weather station to determine the wind direction and speed, too. Record the data in your table. (Pictures A and B)

Picture A

Picture B

4 Make a double-bar graph to show the temperatures and wind speeds recorded at all the locations. Write the wind direction at each location on the appropriate wind-speed bar.

Local Weather Conditions

	1	2	3	4
Location				
Temperature				
Wind Direction				
Wind Speed				

Draw Conclusions

1. Use your table to **compare** the temperature, wind direction, and wind speed at the different locations. What differences, if any, did you find? What conditions were the same?
2. Local weather conditions affect the organisms that live in a location. Do you think wind speed or temperature is more likely to affect living organisms? Explain.
3. Based on your investigation, how would you define the phrase *local weather conditions*?
4. **Scientists at Work** Scientists learn about local weather conditions by **comparing** weather data from different locations. **Draw conclusions** about local weather conditions, based on the locations you studied.

Investigate Further What other factors, in addition to temperature, wind direction, and wind speed, might affect local weather conditions? **Hypothesize** about a factor that might affect local weather conditions. Then **plan and conduct a simple investigation** to test your hypothesis.

Process Skill Tip

You **compare** before you **draw conclusions** about what is the same and what is different about weather conditions in different locations.

LEARN ABOUT

Climates and How They Change

FIND OUT

- what determines a climate
- how human activity can affect climate

VOCABULARY

climate
microclimate
El Niño
greenhouse effect
global warming

Climate

The weather in your area probably changes from day to day and from season to season. Yet year after year many of the same weather conditions are repeated. These repeating conditions, or patterns, make up your area's climate. **Climate** is the average of all weather conditions through all seasons over a period of time. Temperature and precipitation are the major factors that determine climate. Wind speed and direction are also factors.

Temperature is also a major factor of microclimates. A **microclimate** is the climate of a very small area. You probably pass several microclimates on your way to school each day. If you live in a city, you may know that a wooded park has a cooler, wetter climate than a parking lot has. Observing microclimates, as you did in the investigation, is a good way to learn about climates.

These photos of Mount Wheeler, in New Mexico, show different climates on the slope of a high mountain. Notice that, in addition to certain weather conditions, each climate has its own typical plants and animals adapted to living in that climate.

✓ **What is climate?**

At the top of the mountain, you will find a cold, dry climate with few trees or animals. ▼

▲ On the sides of the mountain, the climate is cool and moist, and there are tall trees and forest animals.

▲ At the base of the mountain, the climate is warm and dry. Desert animals and plants such as sagebrush live there.

The coast of northern Maine is covered with snow in the winter. The average daily temperature is in the 20s.

On the Outer Banks of North Carolina, winter temperatures may reach the 40s or 50s.

In Florida the average daily temperature in winter is in the 60s or 70s.

Climate and Latitude

The United States has many different climates. There is the cold, *polar* climate of northern Alaska and the hot, *tropical* climate of Hawai'i and Puerto Rico. Most of the country has more moderate, or *temperate,* climates. But among temperate climates, there are big differences in average temperature and precipitation. Along the East Coast of the United States, for example, average temperatures vary quite a bit—from Florida, in the south, to Maine, in the north. These temperature differences are determined by *latitude,* or the distance a place is from the equator.

Most areas near the equator have tropical climates. There the sun is directly overhead nearly all year, which causes intense heating of the Earth's surface. Farther from the equator, in temperate climates, the sun is directly overhead only part of the year, causing less heating of the Earth's surface. These temperate climates have warm summers but cold winters. Near the poles the sun is never directly overhead. The decreased heating of the Earth's surface at latitudes far from the equator results in cold, polar climates.

In addition to latitude, precipitation causes differences among temperate climates. Most of the East Coast receives a lot of precipitation, allowing thick forests to grow. Farther west there is less precipitation. There are fewer trees and more grasslands, which require less water. Still farther west the grasslands give way to even drier, more desertlike climates that receive very little precipitation.

✔ **Why does Florida have a warmer average temperature than Maine?**

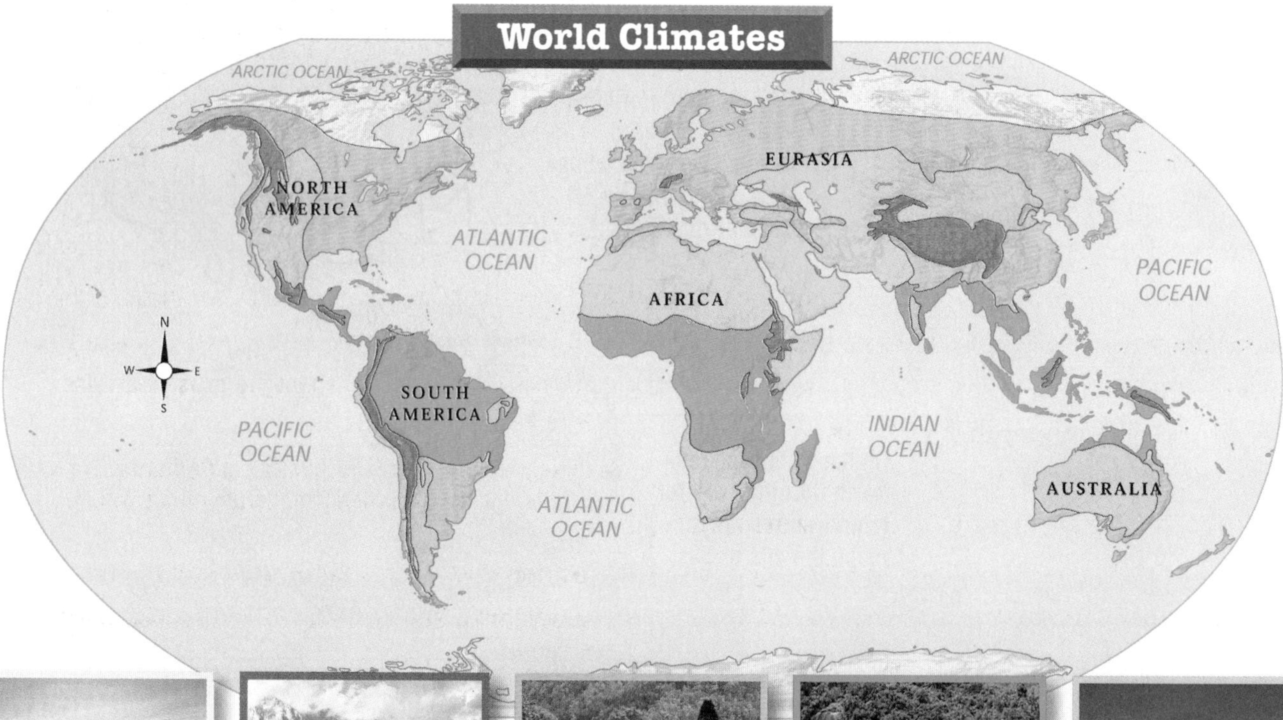

Polar Zone
Cold all year; light precipitation

Mountain Zone
Cold winters, cool summers; moderate to heavy precipitation

Temperate Zone
Cold winters, warm summers; moderate precipitation

Tropical Zone
Hot all year; moderate to heavy precipitation

Desert Zone
Hot summers, cool winters; light precipitation

World Climates

So many factors affect an area's climate that no two places on Earth have exactly the same climate. Anything that affects temperature or precipitation affects climate.

Climate is also affected by prevailing winds. In the United States, the prevailing westerlies help to moderate the hot summer climate by pushing cooling air masses across the country.

Ocean currents can affect climate, too. On the West Coast, the cold California Current flows south from the North Pacific. It keeps the summers cool along the coastal areas of Washington, Oregon, and northern California.

Yet another factor that affects climate is the shape of the land itself. A mountain can have a wet climate on the side facing the prevailing winds and a dry climate on the other side.

Although no two places on Earth have exactly the same climate, Earth's climates can be grouped into five major zones—polar, mountain, temperate, tropical, and desert. Each zone has its own weather patterns and its own typical kinds of life. For example, a polar climate supports small plants and animals like the polar bear. A tropical climate supports lush forests and animals such as monkeys.

✔ **What are the five climate zones?**

Climate Changes

Have you ever heard an older relative say, "When I was young, the winters were much colder than they are now. Why, some days the snow was piled up to the windows."

Your relative may be right. Climate does change over time. Scientists have been measuring the Earth's winds, temperatures, and precipitation for many years. Based on this data and other evidence, they know that Earth's climate is slowly warming. As recently as 50 or 60 years ago, average temperatures in parts of the United States were a degree or two cooler than they are now.

Earth's climate hasn't always been warming up. About 20,000 years ago, Earth was in the middle of an Ice Age. When the climate cools enough, large areas of Earth are covered by sheets of ice, or *glaciers*. Earth has gone through many Ice Ages. During the most recent one, glaciers covered 30 percent of Earth's surface. Evidence of this period can still be seen in the glaciers of Greenland and the Canadian Rockies.

At other times, Earth has had a warmer climate than it does today. Look at the graph to see how Earth's temperature has increased and decreased over time.

▲ One effect of El Niño's heavy rains is mudslides.

▲ During most winters, the weather in California is mild and cool, with only moderate precipitation.

Sometimes Earth's climate changes for just a year or so. The **El Niño** (EL NEEN•yoh) effect is a short-term climate change. Every two to ten years, weather conditions around the Pacific Ocean change dramatically because of changing ocean currents. The normally wet countries of Southeast Asia become dry, while heavy rains fall on the normally dry western coasts of Mexico and California. The photographs above show California during a normal winter and during a winter of heavy El Niño rains.

✔ **What evidence is there that Earth's climate is constantly changing?**

Changes in Earth's temperature might be caused by a change in the size or shape of Earth's orbit or a change in the tilt of Earth's axis.

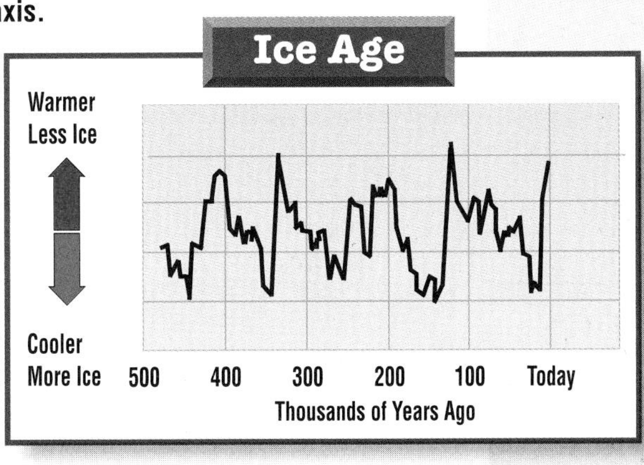

To determine which areas of North America were once covered by ice, scientists look for evidence of glacial erosion and deposition.

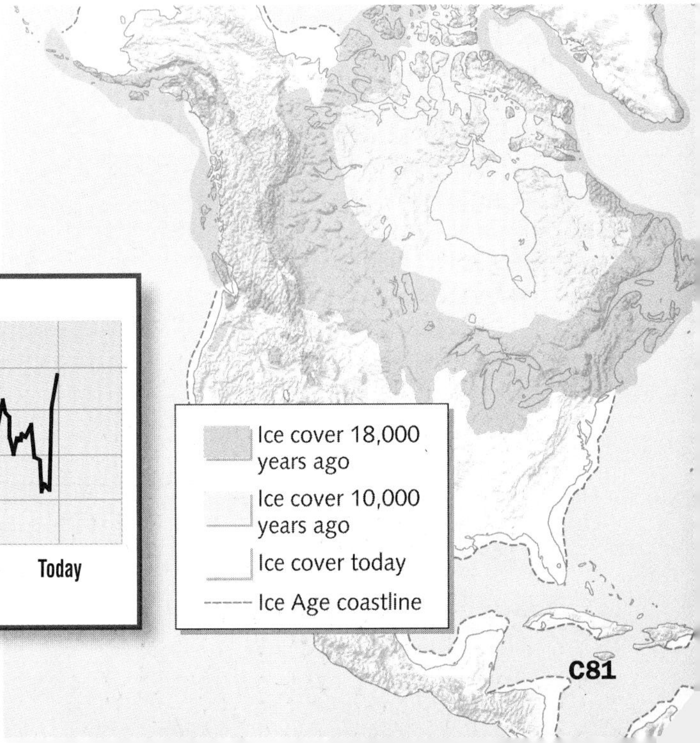

Humans Affect Climate

You know that a city is warmer than the surrounding countryside. In fact, city temperatures may be as much as 8°C (15°F) warmer than surrounding areas. Cities are warmer for several reasons. Buildings, roads, and sidewalks hold heat longer than trees and grass. Cars, buses, and trucks increase city temperatures. Large buildings block winds that might otherwise blow warm air away. All of these factors combine to make a city an area of warm air surrounded by cooler air, or a *heat island.*

Warm air also results from an effect of the burning of fossil fuels such as gasoline. Fossil fuels give off carbon dioxide when burned. Carbon dioxide in the atmosphere absorbs some of the heat given off by Earth. This process, commonly called the **greenhouse effect**, is necessary for life. Without carbon dioxide and other gases in the atmosphere, all of Earth's heat would go off into space, leaving the planet too cold for life. However, too much carbon dioxide in the air may cause climate changes.

Many scientists hypothesize that excess carbon dioxide will lead to **global warming**, an abnormally rapid rise in Earth's average temperature. If Earth's average temperature rises just a few more degrees, the polar icecaps will begin to melt. The melting ice will raise the sea level around the world, flooding many coastal cities.

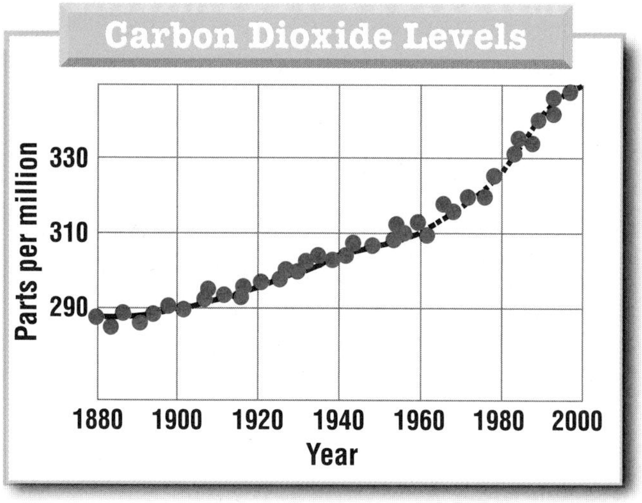

▲ The level of carbon dioxide (CO_2) in the atmosphere has increased over the past century.

▼ Earth's average temperature over the past century has increased at about the same rate.

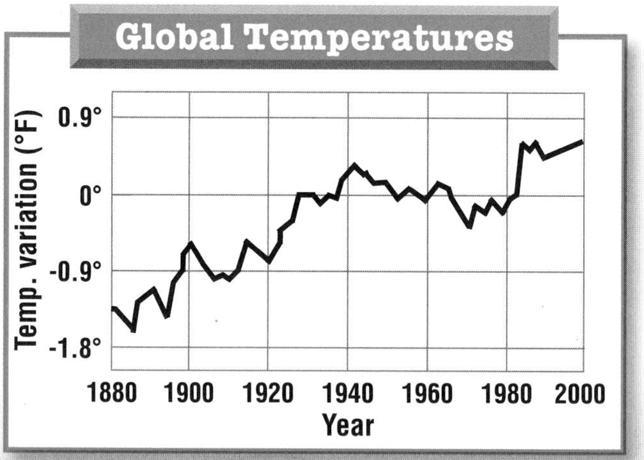

Cities have microclimates that are affected by humans. One reason is that a city has buildings, roads, and vehicles that hold or produce heat.

To reduce this possibility, many countries have agreed to try to reduce the amount of carbon dioxide released into the atmosphere. One way to do this is to burn less fossil fuel.

✔ **What are some ways in which humans affect climate?**

Summary

Climate is the average of all weather conditions through all seasons over a period of time. Temperature and precipitation are the major factors that determine climate. Earth's climate has changed over time as average temperatures have risen and fallen. Human activities, such as burning fossil fuels, can affect climate.

Review

1. What is the difference between climate and microclimate?
2. List four factors that affect climate.
3. What causes an Ice Age?
4. **Critical Thinking** During an Ice Age, what is likely to happen to the levels of oceans around the world?
5. **Test Prep** Burning fossil fuels affects climate by —
   A reducing the number of trees
   B decreasing the amount of sunlight that reaches Earth's surface
   C raising Earth's average temperature
   D changing the prevailing winds

LINKS

MATH LINK

Estimation Look at the graph on page C82 showing global temperature variations. Find the highest and lowest values. Estimate how much Earth's average temperature has varied over the last 100 years.

WRITING LINK

Persuasive Writing—Request Do you think the recent measurements of Earth's temperatures are really evidence of global warming? Write a persuasive letter to the editor of a newspaper, requesting that your point of view be printed. Be sure to include facts to support your point of view.

LITERATURE LINK

Earthmaker's Tales Read *Earthmaker's Tales: North American Indian Stories About Earth Happenings* by Gretchen Will Mayo. Earth and its atmosphere are the subjects of this collection of Native American legends about the origins of thunder, tornadoes, and other weather features.

TECHNOLOGY LINK

Learn more about changes in climate by viewing *El Niño Erosion* and *Global Warming* on the **Harcourt Science Newsroom Video.**

CNN Turner Le@rning

Major Events in Weather Forecasting

In ancient times, weather predictions were based on superstitions. It seemed to make sense that good weather depended on the happiness of the gods. Yet as early as the year 100, Egyptian scientists showed that air expanded when it was heated. This early discovery led to other advances in meteorology, the study of weather.

Observing Weather Systems

In 1735 scientists observed that the sun heated areas near the equator more strongly than areas north or south of the equator. They also discovered that as air above the equator expands, it moves toward the cooler latitudes. This movement results in a global wind pattern, which causes a global weather pattern.

This discovery was followed by the discovery of the "trade winds" north and south of the equator and other wind zones in the Northern Hemisphere. In 1835 French physicist Gustave Coriolis described the movement of air masses north and south of the equator. He showed how winds north or south of the equator curve in different directions. Coriolis realized that these curved air routes were caused by the rotation of Earth.

Modern Forecasting

Wind vanes had long been used to determine wind direction, but it wasn't until the 1600s that instruments were invented that could accurately measure other weather conditions. In 1644 the first barometer was

The History of Weather Forecasting

350 B.C.
Aristotle writes *Meteorologica*, a book about weather observations.

1600
Early weather instruments are invented.

1835
Coriolis discovers what is later called the "Coriolis Effect."

1849
The first weather report sent by telegraph is received by Joseph Henry, secretary of the Smithsonian Institution.

1890
Congress forms an agency called the Weather Bureau, later renamed the National Weather Service.

1902
Scientists discover that the atmosphere has layers. The troposphere and stratosphere are identified.

400 B.C. | A.D. 1600 | A.D. 1700 | A.D. 1800

made. In 1754 G. D. Fahrenheit made the first mercury thermometer.

At least 100 years ago, scientists knew that they could improve their forecasts if they had measurements from enough weather stations around the world. Today there are tens of thousands of weather stations. Each station takes many measurements—temperature, humidity, cloud cover, wind speed and direction, and barometric pressure. Modern communication systems allow scientists to share this information almost instantly. This allows warnings to be issued to people who might be affected by severe weather events.

Weather satellites, first launched in the 1960s, provide the most important data for modern weather forecasting. Satellite data helps scientists understand the global forces that cause local weather conditions. Today countries around the world share satellite weather data.

THINK ABOUT IT

1. What causes winds to curve?
2. What is the most important instrument for weather forecasters today? Explain.

Jacob Bjerknes discovered the warm current, called El Niño, that sometimes produces severe weather along the Pacific coast.

1950s
Bjerknes makes the connection between the El Niño current and certain reversed weather patterns.

1980s
Doppler radar is first used.

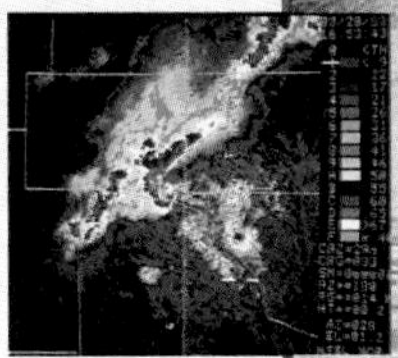

A.D. 1900 — **A.D. 2000**

1960s
The first weather satellites are launched.

1990s
International cooperation and the use of satellites increases understanding of worldwide weather patterns.

Carolyn Kloth

METEOROLOGIST

"A lot of people tend to think that you need to be able to look out of a window to assess the weather. With the use of radar, weather satellites, and all of the other weather data available, you can do the job almost anywhere."

From the time she was in elementary school, Carolyn Kloth knew what she wanted to do—fly airplanes and chase storms. Today Ms. Kloth is doing both of these things as a pilot and a meteorologist at the National Severe Storms Forecast Center in Kansas City, Missouri. She specializes in tracking severe thunderstorms and giving information about them to airplane pilots.

At the severe storms center, Ms. Kloth receives weather data every hour from across North America. The data includes images of cloud patterns, locations of fronts, and the number of lightning strikes. She also studies measurements of air pressure, humidity, precipitation, and temperature, both at the ground and at various levels in the atmosphere. Once all the data has come in, Ms. Kloth uses computers to analyze it. Then she predicts where severe thunderstorms are likely to form across the continent and over nearby coastal waters.

A large storm system

Ms. Kloth issues severe storm warnings to pilots for any storm that has winds of more than 26 m/s, hail larger than 19 mm in diameter, or clouds that may form tornadoes. She finds that about 1 percent of all thunderstorms fit into one or more of those categories. The warnings that Ms. Kloth issues help pilots avoid thunderstorms and result in safer and more comfortable flights.

THINK ABOUT IT

1. How can Ms. Kloth gather weather data without looking out a window?
2. How do you think Ms. Kloth's experience as a pilot helps her in her job at the National Severe Storms Forecast Center?

Air Pressure

How strong is air pressure?

Materials

- plastic sandwich bag
- drinking straw
- tape
- heavy book

Procedure

1. Put one end of the straw in the plastic bag. Then seal the bag shut with tape.
2. Put the plastic bag on a table and lay the book on part of the bag as shown.
3. Blow through the straw into the bag, and observe what happens.

Draw Conclusions

Describe what happened to the bag and the book. Explain what happened. Try to think of a situation where air pressure could be used like this.

Sidewalk Graph

How does sunlight speed up evaporation?

Materials

- sunny sidewalk
- 500 mL water
- chalk
- clock

Procedure

1. Pour about 500 mL of water onto a sidewalk that is in full sunlight.

2. Draw a line around the outside of the puddle with the chalk.
3. Draw a new line around the puddle every 5 min for 20 min.
4. Repeat the experiment on a sidewalk in the shade.

Draw Conclusions

Compare the sizes of the puddles at each 5-min interval. Based on your observations, predict how long it would take for each puddle to evaporate.

Chapter 3 Review and Test Preparation

Vocabulary Review

Use the terms below to complete the sentences. The page numbers in ( ) tell you where to look in the chapter if you need help.

atmosphere (C64)
air pressure (C65)
humidity (C65)
precipitation (C65)
evaporation (C67)
condensation (C67)
local winds (C73)
prevailing winds (C73)
climate (C78)
microclimate (C78)
El Niño (C81)
greenhouse effect (C82)
global warming (C82)

1. Liquid water changes to water vapor through the process of ____. Water vapor turns back into liquid drops of water through the process of ____.
2. Almost all weather occurs in the lowest layer of the ____.
3. Rain or snow is called ____.
4. Water in the air is called ____.
5. The weight of air is known as ____.
6. Global winds that blow constantly from the same direction are known as ____.
7. Winds that depend on local changes in temperature are called ____.
8. The climate of a small area is called a ____.
9. The average of an area's weather conditions through all seasons over a period of time is called ____.
10. Excess carbon dioxide in the atmosphere may lead to ____.
11. The process by which carbon dioxide in the atmosphere absorbs some of the heat given off by Earth is called the ____.
12. One example of a short-term climate change is ____.

Connect Concepts

Copy and complete the idea clusters below, which describe weather and climate.

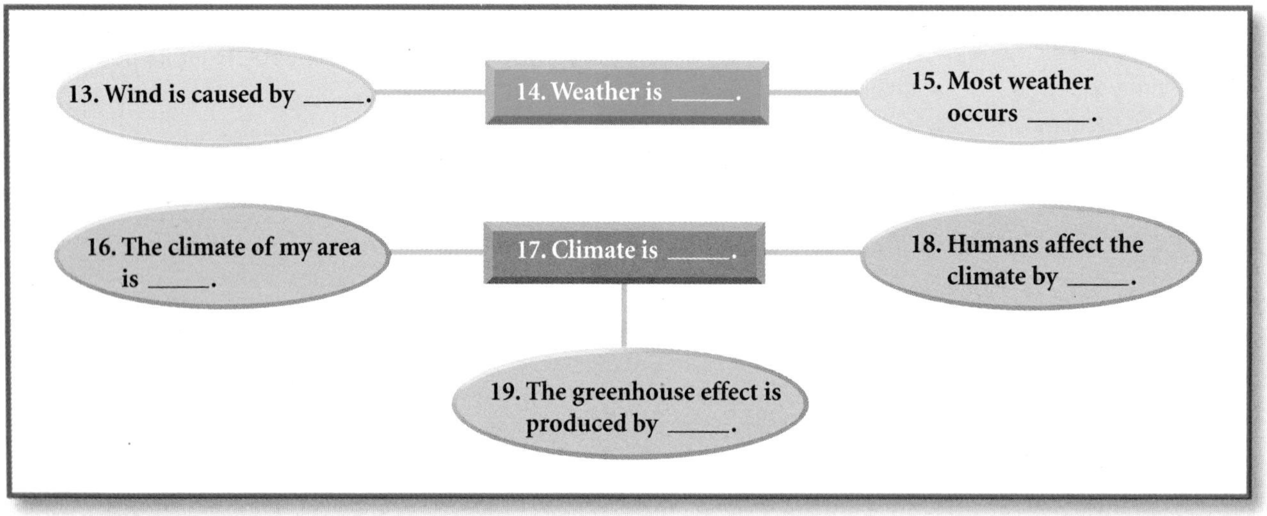

Check Understanding

Write the letter of the best choice.

20. As air warms, —
- **A** air pressure increases
- **B** air pressure decreases
- **C** temperature decreases
- **D** humidity changes

21. A wind vane indicates —
- **F** air pressure
- **G** wind speed
- **H** humidity
- **J** wind direction

22. Wind is caused when air —
- **A** moves from the land to the sea
- **B** moves from the sea to the land
- **C** moves from an area of higher pressure to an area of lower pressure
- **D** moves from an area of lower pressure to an area of higher pressure

23. Prevailing winds are caused by the uneven heating of Earth's atmosphere and by —
- **F** local winds
- **G** air pressure
- **H** Earth's rotation
- **J** temperature

24. Florida has a warmer climate than Maine because Florida —
- **A** is closer to the South Pole
- **B** is closer to the equator
- **C** is nearer to the Atlantic Ocean
- **D** receives more precipitation

25. Most of the eastern United States and the West Coast have a climate that is —
- **F** mountain
- **G** polar
- **H** desert
- **J** temperate

Critical Thinking

26. How does the location of Hawai'i, near the equator, affect its climate?

27. Suppose you live in the middle of the United States and are looking at a weather map. To the north and east of your location, it is raining. To the west and south, the weather is clear. What sort of weather can you expect tomorrow? Explain.

Process Skills Review

28. A thermometer measures air temperature. A barometer measures air pressure. A hygrometer measures humidity, and a rain gauge measures precipitation. Which two of these instruments are most useful for the **measurements** that determine a region's climate? Explain.

29. Which would you **predict** would heat up faster on a sunny day—a pond or a meadow? Explain.

30. **Compare** weather and climate.

Performance Assessment

Your Weather and Climate

Look at a map of the United States. Explain where weather in your area comes from. Describe any local conditions that affect the weather. Then identify the climate zone in which you are located—polar, tropical, temperate, desert, or mountain. Explain what determines your climate zone.

Chapter 4

Exploring the Oceans

If you've ever been to the beach, it may have seemed to you that the water always moves toward the shore. But the movement of ocean water is more complex than that. In addition to causing waves, winds make ocean waters move in great loops around the world.

FAST FACT

In 1947 Thor Heyerdahl crossed the Pacific Ocean on a raft he named *Kon-Tiki.* He wanted to prove that natives of South America could have traveled thousands of miles to the islands of Polynesia by riding on ocean currents.

Vocabulary Preview

- wave
- current
- tide
- shore
- estuary
- headland
- tide pool
- jetty
- scuba
- submersible
- sonar
- desalination

FAST FACT

The deepest spot in Earth's oceans is the Mariana Trench, in the western Pacific. It is 11,334 m (36,198 ft) deep, and was explored in 1960 by the submersible *Trieste III,* shown here. Mount Everest, the highest mountain, is only 8,848 m (29,028 ft) high.

Average Ocean Depths

Ocean	Depth (meters)
Pacific	4,188
Indian	3,872
Atlantic	3,735
Arctic	1,038

FAST FACT

If a bay and a river that empties into it are narrow and shallow, high tides can move rapidly upriver. A wall of water, called a *tidal bore* forms at the front of the tide.

LESSON 1

How Do Ocean Waters Move?

In this lesson, you can . . .

- INVESTIGATE waves.
- LEARN ABOUT the movement of ocean waters.
- LINK to math, writing, language arts, and technology.

INVESTIGATE

Waves

Activity Purpose Have you ever stood on a beach and watched the ocean? If so, you probably noticed that the water is always moving in waves. Waves can also move across a lake or a pond. You can even **observe** very small waves, called ripples, on a puddle. What causes waves? In the investigation, you will **use a model** of the ocean to find out.

Materials

- rectangular pan
- water
- straw

Activity Procedure

1. **Make a model** of the ocean by half-filling the pan with water. (Picture A)
2. Place your straw near one side of the pan, and gently blow across the surface of the water. What happens? (Picture B)

◀ Wind and waves work together to make windsurfing an exciting sport.

Picture A

Picture B

3. **Observe** the height and speed of the waves you make. **Record** your observations.

4. Repeat Step 2 several times, blowing a little harder each time. What do you **observe** about the waves you make? **Record** your observations.

Draw Conclusions

1. Use your observations to describe the relationship between how hard you blow and the height and speed of the waves.
2. From what you observed in this activity, what can you **infer** about the cause of waves on oceans and other bodies of water?
3. **Scientists at Work** Scientists often **use models** to learn about things they cannot **observe** directly. What did your model help you observe about waves?

Investigate Further **Predict** how high the waves on a pond, a lake, or the ocean will be on a calm day and on a stormy day. Then test your predictions by **using a model**.

Process Skill Tip

Observing is the most basic science skill. You **observe** when you use your senses to note the properties of an object or event, such as the effect of moving air on water.

LEARN ABOUT

How Ocean Waters Move

FIND OUT

- how waves move
- what causes ocean currents
- what causes tides

VOCABULARY

wave
current
tide

Wind and Waves

The waters of the ocean never stop moving. Most of the movement of water on the ocean's surface is due to waves. A **wave** is the up-and-down movement of surface water.

In the investigation you observed that wind produces waves. In fact, most waves are caused by wind. When wind blows over the surface of a body of water, it causes the surface of the water to move with it. Because water moves more slowly than air, the water piles up, forming a ripple. The wind then pushes on the side of the ripple, making it grow in height, and turning the ripple into a wave.

In the investigation you also observed that the height of a wave is related to how hard the wind blows. On a calm day, ocean waves may be less than 1.5 m (about 5 ft) high. But during a storm, waves can reach heights of 30 m (about 100 ft). That's as high as a ten-story building!

Even though the water in a wave may rise and fall by as much as 30 m, very little of the water moves forward. What moves across the ocean's surface is energy. Think about this: When you shake a rope, the rope moves up and down or side to side as waves travel to the

Water in a wave moves in circles, returning to about the place where it started. ▼

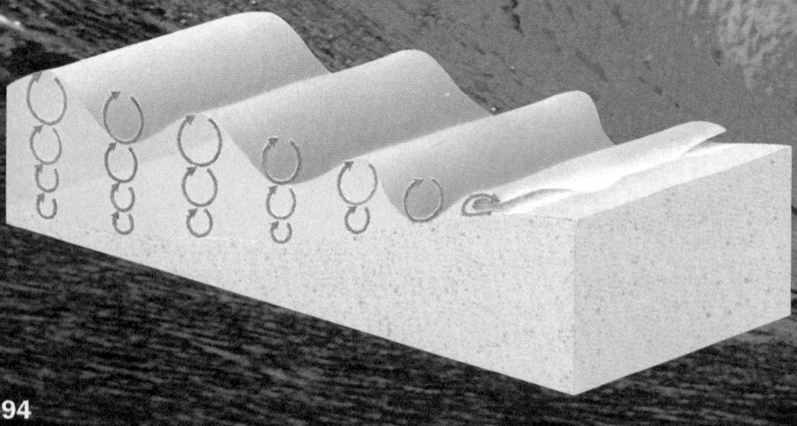

end of the rope. But the rope itself doesn't move forward. This motion is similar to what happens to water in the ocean. The waves move across the surface of the water, but the water stays in almost the same place.

✔ **What causes most waves in water?**

Hurricane winds produce huge waves that East Coast surfers enjoy before the storm arrives.

Other Kinds of Waves

Most ocean waves are caused by wind. But some waves can be caused by earthquakes and volcanoes, extremely low air pressure, or several things acting together.

Some of the biggest waves in the oceans are caused by earthquakes and volcanoes. These giant waves are called *tsunamis* (soo•NAH•meez). In the deep ocean, a tsunami may be more than 100 km (about 62 mi) long but less than 1 m (about 3 ft) high. These waves pass under ships without being noticed. But when a tsunami reaches a shore, friction with the ocean bottom slows the wave. This causes the wave to grow to as much as 25 m (about 82 ft), destroying everything in its path.

During hurricanes and tropical storms, large domes of water called *storm surges* form. Low air pressure at the storm's center causes ocean water to rise. Strong winds form huge waves on top of the storm surge, and they push this high water ahead of the storm. If the storm is moving toward land, it may send a wall of water up to 10 m (about 33 ft) high crashing onto the beach.

Another kind of wave is called a rogue (ROHG) wave. This is a huge wave, much higher than the waves around it. Many rogue waves form when large storm waves join together.

✔ **Name three different kinds of waves, and tell what causes them.**

Tsunamis, such as the one that hit Hilo, Hawai'i, in 1946, cause great damage to buildings along the shore. ▼

Even large boats can be sunk by rogue waves. ▼

Currents

Although waves are the most easily seen kind of ocean movement, currents move much more water. An ocean **current** is a stream of water that flows like a river through the ocean. Unlike waves, currents actually move water forward, sometimes for long distances.

Large ocean currents, known as *surface currents,* flow across the surface of the oceans. Surface currents are usually caused by prevailing winds. As a prevailing wind blows across the surface of the ocean, the water begins to move as a stream. Some surface currents can be hundreds of kilometers wide and hundreds of meters deep. A single one of these "ocean rivers" can move more water than the Amazon, the largest river in the world.

A surface current can carry cold water to warm regions. It can also carry warm water to cold regions. One surface current is the Gulf Stream. This warm current flows northeast from the Caribbean Sea, past the East Coast of the United States, and across the North Atlantic. Even after its long trip across the cold Atlantic, there is enough warm water in this current to warm the climate of Great Britain and northern Europe. That's why palm trees can grow along the southern coast of England.

The warm waters of the Gulf Stream are shown in orange and red in this satellite photograph. Colder waters are shown in green and blue. ▼

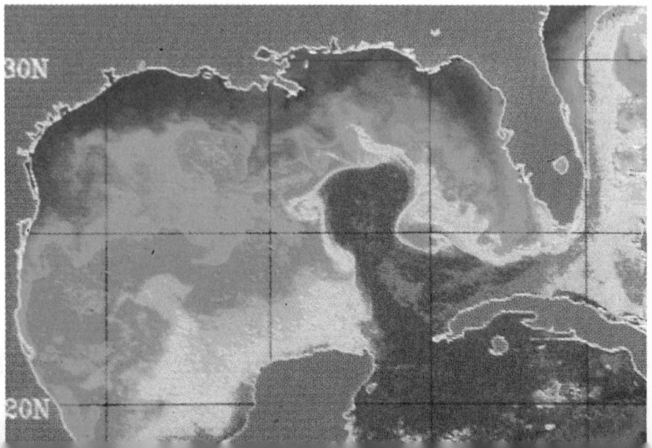

▲ Rip currents (red arrows) may flow away from a beach at 8 km/h (about 5 mi/h). If you get caught in a rip current, swim parallel to the shore until you move out of the current. The water on both sides of the rip current flows toward the beach.

Surface currents aren't the only currents flowing through the oceans. *Shoreline currents* are local currents that run along the coast. Local winds and shifting beach materials may cause shoreline currents to change from day to day.

A *rip current* is a shoreline current that flows away from the beach. A rip current is often caused by a sand spit, a long ridge of sand that forms offshore near a beach. Ocean waves flow over the sand spit and toward the beach. But water from the waves can't flow back over the sand spit. The water piles up, trapped by the sand spit, until a small break opens up in the sand spit. The water then flows rapidly out through the opening, producing a strong current.

When waves strike a shore at an angle, they move water forward along the shore. This movement of water parallel to the beach produces another type of shoreline current, called a longshore current. Longshore currents carry large amounts of beach materials from one place to another.

Surface Currents

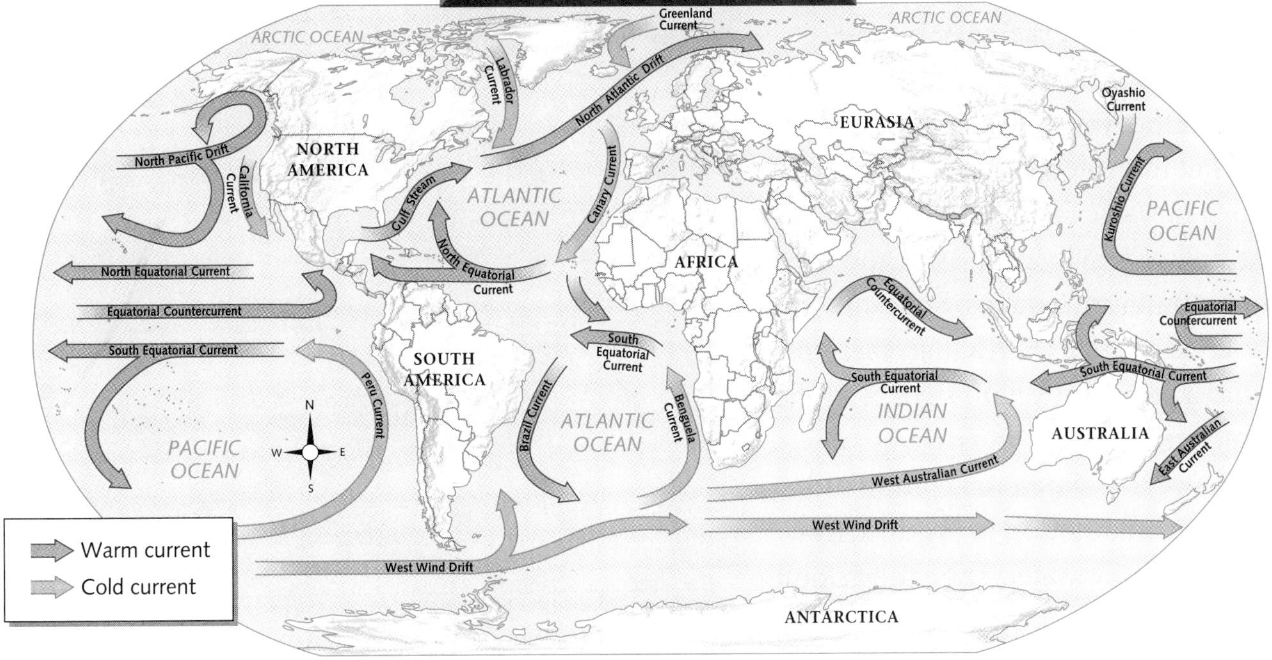

▲ This diagram shows how surface currents move. The red arrows show warm water, and the blue arrows show cold water.

Although wind blowing across the surface of an ocean can produce currents, these currents don't continue moving in the same direction as the wind. Earth's rotation causes ocean currents to bend to the right in the Northern Hemisphere and to the left in the Southern Hemisphere. The currents start moving in giant circles.

Not all ocean currents are caused by wind. Deep-ocean currents are caused by differences in water temperature. Cold water is heavier than warm water, so it sinks. The cold water then flows along the bottom of the ocean.

✓What causes ocean currents?

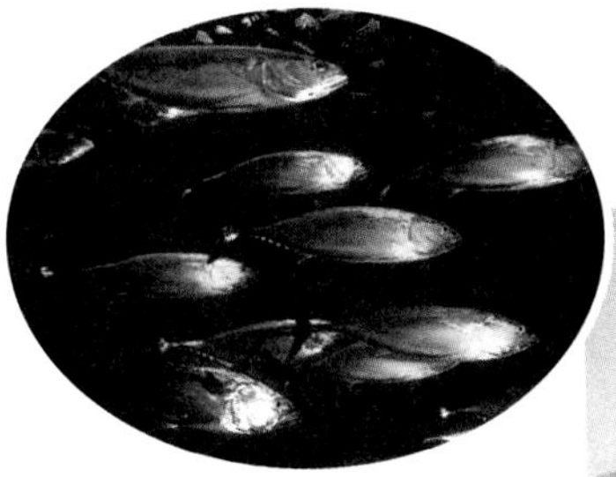

▲ As a deep-ocean current rises to the surface, it carries nutrients that can support large amounts of sea life.

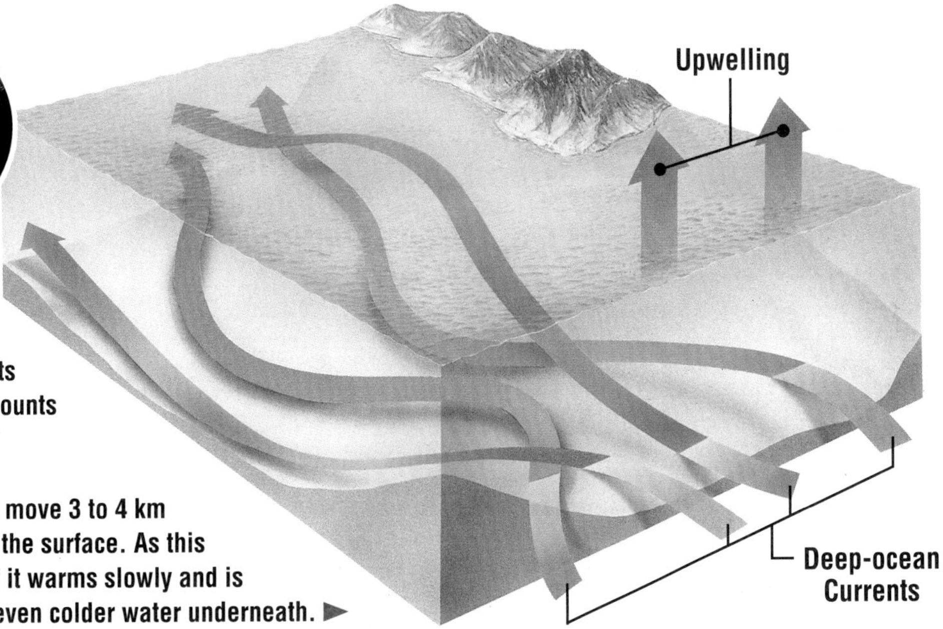

Cold deep-ocean currents move 3 to 4 km (about 2 to 3 mi) beneath the surface. As this cold water flows, some of it warms slowly and is pushed to the surface by even colder water underneath. ▶

Tides

Once or twice each day, ocean water rises and falls at every beach around the world. This repeated rise and fall in the level of the ocean is called the **tide**. Tides are caused by the pull of gravity of the sun and the moon on Earth's waters. Since the moon is closer to Earth than the sun, it has a greater effect on tides than the sun does.

The pull of the moon combines with Earth's rotation to produce traveling bulges of water. The moon's pull on the oceans is strongest on the side of Earth facing the moon. This causes Earth's shape to become slightly oval. Solid parts of Earth change very little. But the oceans bulge out on the side of Earth nearest the moon and on the side farthest from the moon. As Earth rotates, it pulls these bulges along.

The bulges of water on either side of Earth are called *high tides*. Low-water levels between high tides are called *low tides*. Most coastal areas have one or two low tides and one or two high tides every 24 hours. Low and high tides occur at regular times, which can be predicted. The table shows high and

▲ **Very high tides occur every 14 days when the moon and sun line up. Weaker tides occur when the moon, the sun, and the Earth form a right angle.**

In the Bay of Fundy, between Maine and Nova Scotia, the difference between high and low tides can be as much as 20 m (about 66 ft)!

Tides for the Bay of Fundy

Date	Time	Ht.	Time	Ht.	Time	Ht.	Time	Ht.
1/15/1999	0354	5.4	1003	24.7	1623	3.8	2232	23.6
1/16/1999	0437	4.8	1045	25.2	1705	3.3	2313	24.1
1/17/1999	0519	4.4	1126	25.6	1746	2.8	2354	24.5
1/18/1999	0600	4.0	1206	25.9	1826	2.4		
1/19/1999	0034	24.8	0642	3.7	1247	26.0	1908	2.2
1/20/1999	0115	25.0	0725	3.5	1329	26.0	1950	2.2
1/21/1999	0158	25.1	0810	3.5	1414	25.7	2035	2.4

low tides during one week in Canada's Bay of Fundy. The Bay of Fundy is famous for its extremely high and low tides, so knowing when tides will occur is very important for boaters.

✔ **What causes tides?**

Summary

The ocean is in constant motion. Ocean waters move as waves, currents, and tides. Most waves are caused by wind. Currents are streams of water caused by winds or differences in water temperature. Tides are caused by the gravitational pull of the moon and sun on Earth's oceans.

Review

1. How does the water in an ocean wave move?
2. Compare the causes of surface currents with those of deep-ocean currents.
3. How do the moon's gravity and Earth's rotation affect tides?
4. **Critical Thinking** For a science fair project, a student dissolves food coloring in a cup of cold water. Then the student pours the cold, colored water into a glass of warm water. **Predict** what will happen to the colored water. Explain your prediction.
5. **Test Prep** Tides are caused by —
   A ocean currents
   B waves and the prevailing winds
   C the gravitational pull of the moon and sun on the oceans
   D hurricanes and other tropical storms

LINKS

MATH LINK

Calculate Look at the tide table on page C98. Find the tides for January 20. At what times will high tide occur on that day? About how many hours apart are the two high tides?

WRITING LINK

Narrative Writing—Story Do some research about an ocean current. Where does the current begin? Where does it go? What does the current carry? How does the current affect the lands it touches? Then write a short story for your teacher about the current.

LANGUAGE ARTS LINK

Editing After you finish the first draft of your story about an ocean current, trade stories with a classmate for comments and corrections. Mark any errors in spelling or grammar. Then look for parts of the story that you like. Look also for parts that could be more exciting or that need to be explained better. Write any comments on the manuscript and give it back to your classmate.

TECHNOLOGY LINK

Learn more about the effects of waves and currents by visiting this Smithsonian Institution Internet site.
www.si.edu/harcourt/science

Smithsonian Institution®

LESSON 2

How Do Oceans Interact with the Land?

In this lesson, you can . . .

INVESTIGATE the effect of waves on a beach.

LEARN ABOUT how the oceans affect the shoreline.

LINK to math, writing, technology, and other areas.

INVESTIGATE

The Effect of Waves on a Beach

Activity Purpose Every day ocean waves keep pounding against the shore. How do waves change a shore? In this activity you will **make a model** so you can **observe** the effect of waves on a beach.

Materials

- stream table
- sand
- water

Activity Procedure

1. Use sand to **make a model** of a beach at one end of the stream table. The beach should have a gentle slope. (Picture A)
2. Slowly add water to the stream table until it is about half full. Try not to disturb the beach.

◀ Ocean waves will soon destroy this sand castle.

Picture A

Picture B

3. Make a wave by lifting the sand end of the stream table about 2 cm above the tabletop and then dropping it. What do you **observe** about the beach and the water? Repeat this several times. **Record** your observations.

4. Repeat Steps 1–3, but this time build a beach that is much steeper than the first one. **Record** your observations. (Picture B)

Draw Conclusions

1. Use your observations to explain how waves affect a beach.
2. Does the slope of the beach matter? Explain.
3. **Scientists at Work** Scientists often **make a model** to study how natural processes work. How did your model help you **observe** how waves affect a beach? What couldn't you observe about wave action with your model?

Investigate Further If possible, study the shore of a pond, a lake, or an ocean in your area. What do you **observe** about the shore? What questions do you have about how waves affect the shore? **Plan and conduct a simple investigation** to help you answer your questions. Decide what equipment you will need to use in your investigation.

Process Skill Tip

Not everyone can **observe** firsthand the effect of waves. But you can **make a model** to help you understand just how waves affect a beach.

How Ocean Waters Shape the Shore

FIND OUT

- how ocean waves and currents shape the shore
- how human activities can change the shore

VOCABULARY

shore
estuary
headland
tide pool
jetty

At the Shore

The area from where waves begin to break to the highest place they reach on the beach is called the shore. The **shore** is the area where the ocean and land meet and interact. Anyone who has lived near the ocean knows that the shore is a place of constant change.

As you saw in the investigation, waves change the shore in several ways. One is by grinding pebbles and rocks against the shore. This action erodes the bottoms of cliffs, causing them to break apart and fall into the ocean. Another way waves change the shore is through water pressure. Each breaking wave hurls tons of water at the shore. This water pressure loosens pebbles and small rocks, which the outgoing waves carry into the ocean. Finally, because seawater is a weak acid, it slowly dissolves rock along the shore.

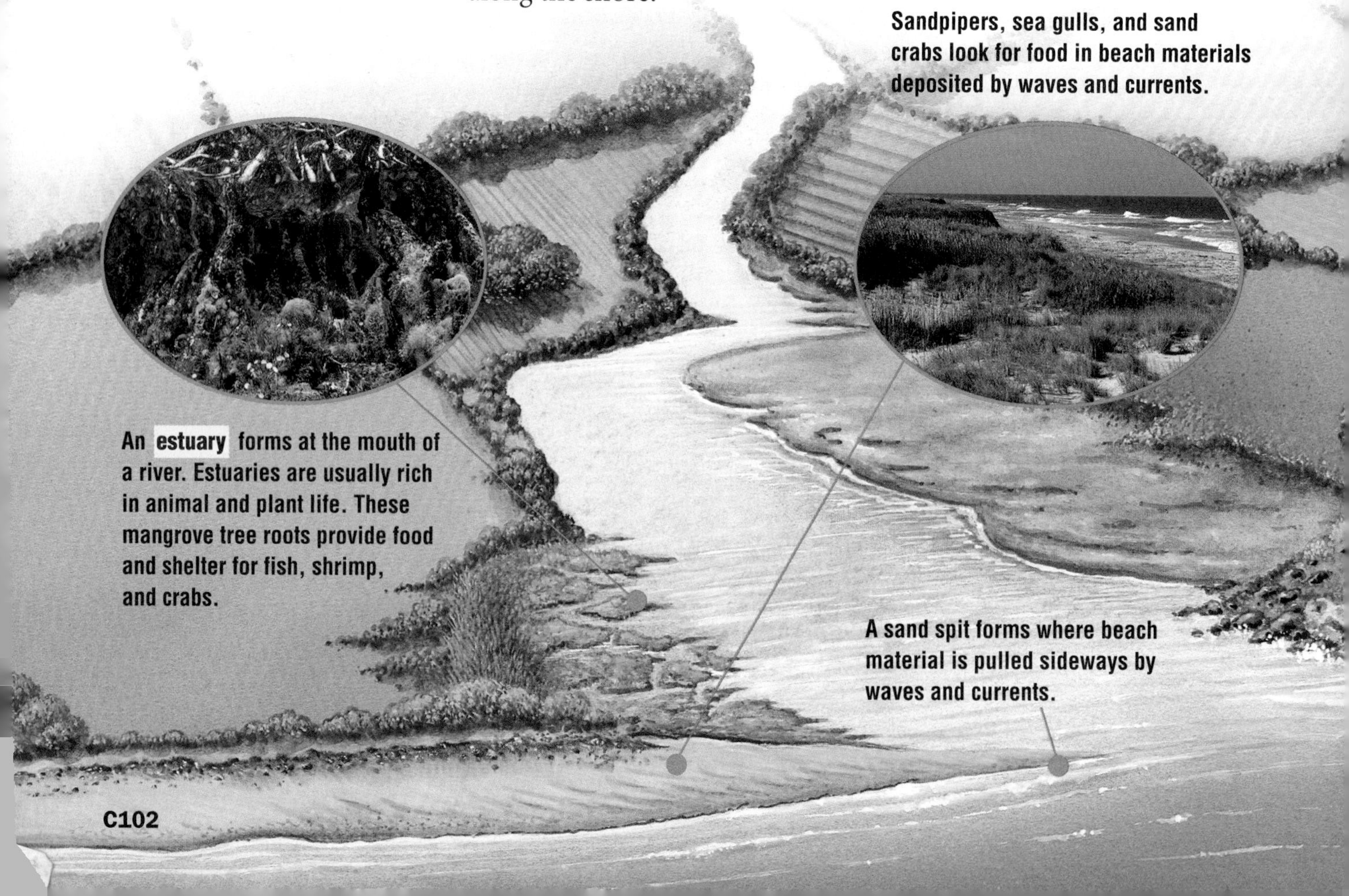

Sandpipers, sea gulls, and sand crabs look for food in beach materials deposited by waves and currents.

An **estuary** forms at the mouth of a river. Estuaries are usually rich in animal and plant life. These mangrove tree roots provide food and shelter for fish, shrimp, and crabs.

A sand spit forms where beach material is pulled sideways by waves and currents.

Where a shore is made of both soft rock and hard rock, erosion is uneven. Soft rock erodes faster than hard rock. Wave action may destroy the soft rock, forming small bays like those shown below. As the soft rock is washed away, the hard rock may be left as a rocky point, or **headland**. Sometimes the ocean cuts sea caves into a headland. If waves continue to erode the sea caves, a sea arch may form.

Currents also change a shore. If you've ever been swimming in the ocean, you may have noticed that when you came out of the water, you had to walk up and along the beach to the place where you left your towel. A longshore current carried you down the beach.

Longshore currents also move sand, pebbles, and shells along the shore. In places where the shore changes direction, a longshore current slows down and deposits beach materials. A new beach is formed, or the existing beach receives new sand and pebbles.

✓ **How do waves and currents change the shore?**

A tide pool is a pool of seawater found along a rocky shoreline. At high tide the pool is under water. This tide pool in California provides a habitat for a great variety of plants and animals.

Two sea caves have further eroded to form a sea arch like this one on Anacapa Island, in Channel Islands National Park, California.

Human Activities Affect the Shore

Human activities also change the shore. People in coastal communities often build structures to protect their beaches from erosion. These structures can block longshore currents and change the natural processes that erode and build up a shore.

At Cape Hatteras, along the coast of North Carolina, the Atlantic Ocean has eroded the beach so much that the lighthouse there was in danger of falling into the sea. The Cape Hatteras Lighthouse is one of the most famous lighthouses in the United States. To save the lighthouse, three jetties were built along the water's edge to catch sand and build up the beach. A **jetty** is a wall-like structure made of rocks that sticks out into the ocean.

A jetty protects a beach by trapping sand and pebbles that normally flow down the coast with the longshore current. But jetties can also harm beaches. Although the beach the jetty protects receives extra sand, beaches down the shore may lose their supply of sand and actually erode faster.

Cape Hatteras Lighthouse is safe for now. The lighthouse was moved farther from the ocean in 1999.

✓ How do human activities affect the shore?

These jetties were built to protect this beach from erosion. ▼

The Cape Hatteras Lighthouse was built in 1870 after many ships had sunk in the so-called Graveyard of the Atlantic. ▼

This was the Cape Hatteras Lighthouse in 1998. On parts of Hatteras Island, ocean waves wash away 4.3 m (about 15 ft) of beach each year. ►

Summary

The shore is changed by waves, currents, and human activities. Waves erode beaches and cliffs. Longshore currents deposit beach materials such as sand, pebbles, and shells along the shore. Jetties and other structures can affect the natural processes of shore change.

Review

1. How do waves erode beaches and cliffs?
2. How does a longshore current affect the shore?
3. What are two ways in which a jetty can affect a shore?
4. **Critical Thinking** A pier is built sticking out into the ocean. After a few years, sand builds up along one side of the pier. Explain why.
5. **Test Prep** An estuary is an area rich in plant and animal life that forms —
   A along a sandbar
   B along a jetty
   C at a headland
   D at the mouth of a river

Padre Island, Texas, is a wide, beautiful barrier island. A barrier island is a long ridge of sand in the ocean running parallel to the shore. A barrier island gets its name from the fact that it blocks ocean waves and storm surges, protecting the low coastal mainland.

LINKS

MATH LINK

Estimation The Atlantic Ocean is eroding parts of Hatteras Island at the rate of 4.3 m per year. Estimate how many years it will take for 30 m of the island to be eroded.

WRITING LINK

Persuasive Writing—Opinion Take a stand for or against building jetties to save a beach. Prepare notes for a short speech explaining your point of view. Be sure to include facts and drawings or photographs to support your position. Present your speech to your classmates.

ART LINK

Shore Diagram Draw a picture showing how the ocean both erodes and builds up beaches.

SOCIAL STUDIES LINK

Shore Map Find a shore in your state to map. If you don't live near an ocean, map a large lake. Show natural features such as bays, estuaries, and beaches.

TECHNOLOGY LINK

Learn more about the interactions of the ocean and the shore by visiting this Smithsonian Institution Internet site.
www.si.edu/harcourt/science

Smithsonian Institution®

LESSON 3

How Do People Explore the Oceans and Use Ocean Resources?

In this lesson, you can . . .

- INVESTIGATE how scientists measure ocean depths.
- LEARN ABOUT how people explore the oceans and use ocean resources.
- LINK to math, writing, literature, and technology.

This copper diving helmet was first used in about 1819. ▶

INVESTIGATE

How Scientists Measure Ocean Depths

Activity Purpose In 1521 Portuguese explorer Ferdinand Magellan tried to measure the depth of the Pacific Ocean. He dropped 730 m (about 2400 ft) of weighted rope over the side of his ship. But this wasn't nearly enough rope to reach the bottom of the ocean. Today's scientists use *sonar*, or sound wave devices, to determine how deep the ocean is. In this activity you will learn about two ways to **measure** the depth of water—Magellan's way and a more modern way.

Materials

- shoe box
- sand, pebbles, small rocks
- construction paper
- ruler
- string
- weight
- calculator

Activity Procedure

1. **Make a model** of the ocean floor by pouring sand and pebbles into the shoe box. Then scatter a few small rocks on top of the sand. (Picture A)
2. Cut a piece of construction paper large enough to cover the top of the box. This will stand for the sea surface.
3. With a pencil and ruler, draw a grid on the paper 4 squares wide by 8 squares long. Number the squares 1 through 32, and tape the lid onto the box. Tie the weight to a piece of string about twice as long as the box is deep.

4. Make a hole in the first square in any row and lower the weighted end of the string until the weight just touches the ocean floor. (Picture A)

5. Hold the string at sea level. **Measure** the length of string you pinched off to find the depth of the ocean. **Record** your measurement. Repeat Steps 4 and 5 for the remaining squares in that row.

6. Now copy the Sonar Data table. The "Time" is the number of seconds it takes for a sound to travel from a boat to the bottom of the ocean and back to the boat.

7. Use a calculator to multiply the Location 1 time by 1500 m/s (the speed of sound in water). Then divide the product by 2. This number is the depth of the water in meters at Location 1. This one has been done for you.

8. Repeat Step 7 for each location in the table. Then make a line graph of the depths. The graph will be a profile of the ocean floor.

Picture A

Sonar Data

Location	Time (s)	Depth (m)
1	1.8	1350
2	2.0	
3	3.6	
4	4.5	
5	5.3	
6	2.3	
7	3.1	
8	4.6	
9	5.0	
10	5.2	

Draw Conclusions

1. Why do you think scientists today use sonar rather than weighted ropes to **measure** the depth of the ocean?
2. When using sonar, why must you divide each product by 2 to calculate the depth of the water?
3. **Scientists at Work** How could a scientist use sonar to **measure** the size of large objects on the ocean floor?

Investigate Further How could you find the depth of a pond, lake, or river? **Plan and conduct a simple investigation** to find out. Select the equipment you would need to use.

Process Skill Tip

You **measure** when you use a tool to find how deep the water is.

LEARN ABOUT

Exploring the Oceans and Using Ocean Resources

FIND OUT

- about ocean exploration
- about *Alvin*, the submersible that helped find RMS *Titanic*
- how people use ocean resources

VOCABULARY

scuba
submersible
sonar
desalination

Exploring the Ocean

Did you know that more than 70 percent of Earth is covered with water? Viewed from space, the continents we live on seem like big islands with oceans around them. People have been exploring the oceans for thousands of years. Early peoples took trips in small boats to search for food, to move to new homes, and to find better trade routes. Some went just for adventure. The time line below shows some of the ways in which people have explored the oceans in the past 600 years.

Scientists and explorers have been studying the oceans for hundreds of years. People designed diving suits as early as the

The voyage of HMS *Challenger* in 1872 started the modern science of oceanography (oh•shuhn•AWG•ruh•fee)—the scientific study of the oceans.

1400s	1500s	1600s	1700s	1800s

This diving suit was designed in the 1400s.

Sir Edmond Halley, an English astronomer, built this diving bell in 1690. Air was sent down to the bell using barrels and leather tubes. The bell shape trapped air for the divers to use.

1400s, and by 1690, divers could use Sir Edmond Halley's diving bell to explore to a depth of 18 m (about 60 ft) below sea level.

Detailed studies of the oceans began in 1872 with the voyage of the British ship HMS *Challenger.* Led by C. Wyville Thomson, six scientists spent more than three years at sea. They took thousands of samples and measurements of the oceans. They studied the chemistry of sea water and collected ocean plants, animals, and minerals.

With simple methods like you used in the investigation, Thomson and his staff achieved many firsts. Using a weighted line and a steam engine, they measured a water depth of 8185 m (about 26,850 ft) in the western Pacific. They also captured and classified 4717 new species of marine life. The scientific reports of their expedition filled 50 books.

Today's scientists use many different technologies to explore the oceans. They dive beneath the water wearing **scuba** equipment. (The letters *s-c-u-b-a* stand for ***s**elf-**c**ontained **u**nderwater **b**reathing **a**pparatus.*) They travel in small, underwater vehicles called **submersibles**. Satellites are used to study ocean currents from space, and **sonar** (a device that uses sound waves) is used to map the ocean floor.

✓ What technologies do scientists use to explore the oceans?

In 1960 Jacques Piccard and Donald Walsh went down in the *Trieste II* to the deepest place in the Pacific Ocean. They reached a depth of 10,920 m (about 35,800 ft). At this depth the top of Mount Everest would still be about 1525 m (5000 ft) below the ocean's surface.

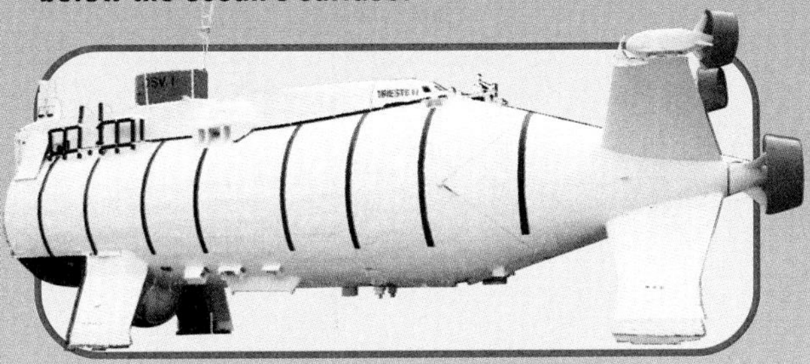

Today, satellites can measure an ocean's salt content, temperature, wave heights, and current flows from thousands of kilometers in space. Sensors can even show where tiny organisms called plankton are found in ocean waters.

1900–1935 | 1935–1960 | 1960–2000

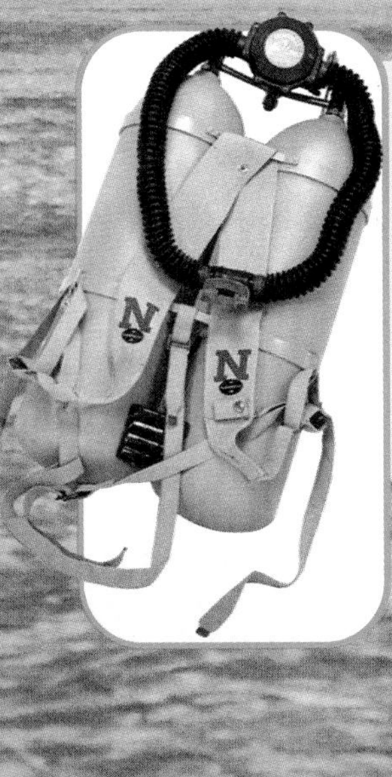

The Aqua-lung, an early form of scuba, was invented in 1942 by French explorer Jacques Cousteau. With scuba gear, a diver can move freely about underwater to a depth of about 60 m (200 ft).

The submersible *Alvin* has played an important role in exploring ocean depths. To reach the *Titanic* in 1986, it had to travel nearly 4000 m (about 13,000 ft) beneath the ocean's surface.

Submersibles

One of the best-known submersibles is *Alvin*, named in honor of ocean scientist Allyn Vine. In 1956 Vine convinced the United States government that scientists needed deep-diving vessels that could hold small crews. By the 1960s *Alvin* was exploring the oceans.

In 1977 scientists in *Alvin* discovered underwater vents along the Mid-Atlantic Ridge. In 1986 *Alvin* was used to explore the wreckage of the sunken ship RMS *Titanic.*

Alvin may have been the first submersible to explore *Titanic,* but it wasn't the last. During the 1990s a team of French and American explorers used a newer submersible, *Nautile,* to continue the job *Alvin* started.

Nautile first visited the *Titanic* wreck in 1987, bringing up some objects from the site. In the 1990s even more objects were brought up, including a large part of the sunken ship itself.

THE INSIDE STORY

Alvin

Alvin **is launched from a surface ship. The submersible has made thousands of dives, each lasting about nine hours.**

In 1977, scientists in *Alvin* discovered hot springs deep under the ocean. The springs come from vents in the ocean floor over volcanically active areas.

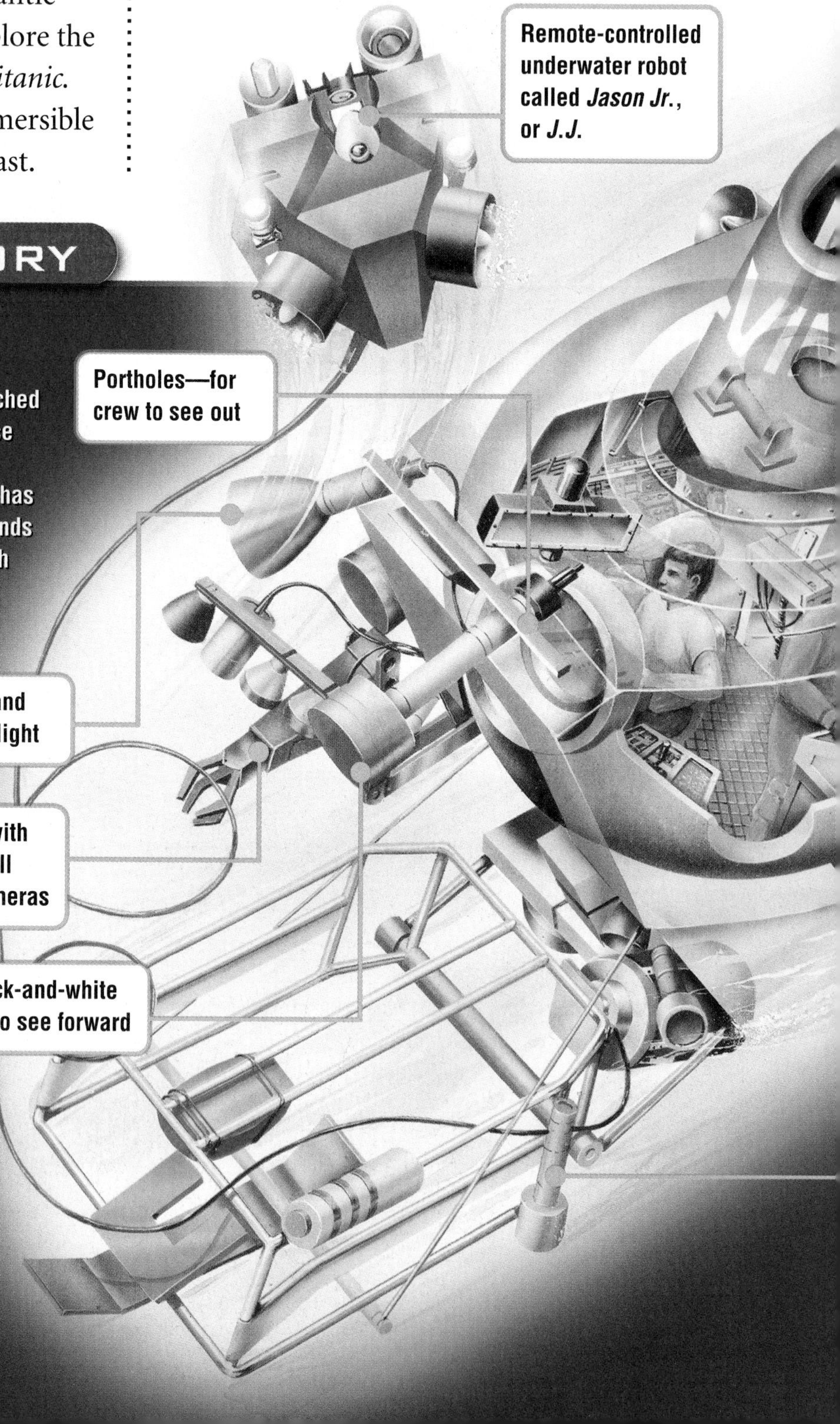

With space for crews of three—one pilot and two scientists each—*Alvin* and *Nautile* can work inside sea caves, shipwrecks, and other small spaces.

Crewed submersibles allow scientists to observe underwater objects up close. They have been able to make important scientific discoveries, as well as explore sunken ships.

But in the future, underwater exploration may be done with small, crewless submersibles. These underwater robots can fit into places too small for *Alvin* or *Nautile.* And they can dive deeper and stay longer on the ocean floor.

✔ **What kinds of places have scientists used submersibles to explore?**

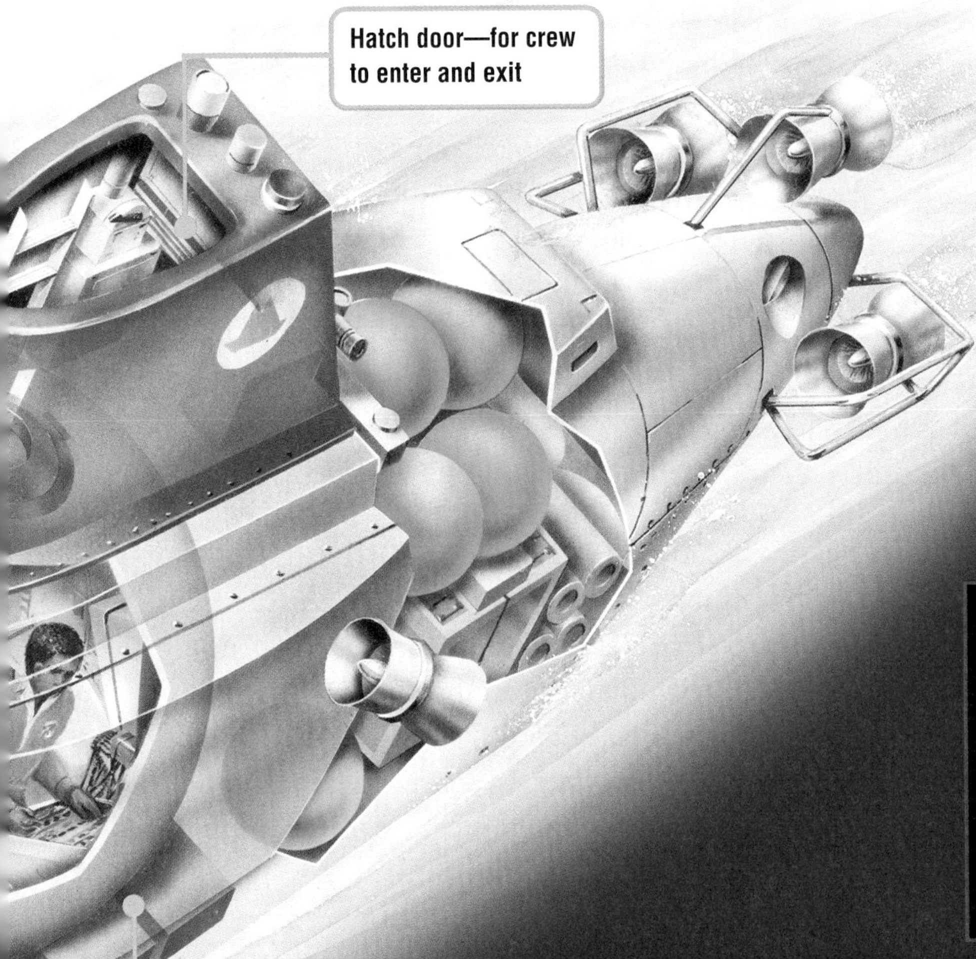

In 1986 a team of scientists led by Dr. Robert Ballard used *Alvin* to go down to the wreck of the *Titanic*. They explored the remains of the sunken ocean liner and took the first photographs of the ship since it sank in 1912.

This photograph shows a chandelier before the *Titanic*'s first—and only—voyage. In 1912 the *Titanic* struck an iceberg in the North Atlantic and sank to the bottom of the ocean.

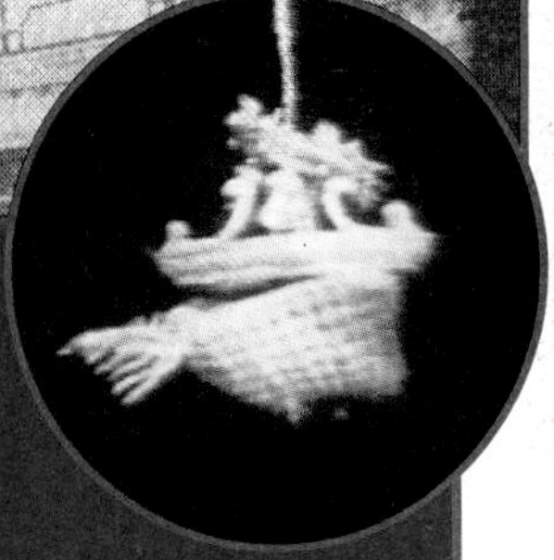

The same chandelier was filmed nearly 75 years later by a remote-controlled robot named *J.J.* The robot is attached to *Alvin* by a 61-m (about 200-ft) cable. With *J.J.*, scientists can "see" places too small or too dangerous for *Alvin* to enter.

Using Ocean Resources

The importance of the oceans is not just in the discoveries they hold for scientists. The oceans contain huge amounts of natural resources. Ocean waters are filled with plants and animals. The ocean floor contains many minerals. Gas and oil are buried deep beneath the ocean floor. And in some places, sea water itself has become an important resource.

Among the ocean's most important resources are its fish and shellfish. Millions of people around the world feed their families by fishing from small boats. Others fish for large companies on factory ships—huge boats where fish can be cleaned, processed, and canned or frozen right on board.

Sea plants are another ocean resource. People eat some kinds of seaweed as food. Carrageenin (kar•uh•JEE•nuhn), a product made from seaweed, is used in foods, toothpaste, hand creams, and fertilizer.

As resources on land become scarce, people are beginning to mine underwater mineral deposits. Sand, gravel, and shells are easily obtained near the shore. Hundreds of millions of tons are dredged from the sea each year and used for road construction and building materials. Minerals containing iron, copper, manganese, nickel, and cobalt can be taken from lumps, or nodules, lying on the sea floor. These deep-sea nodules are difficult to mine, however, since they are located at depths of 4000 m (about 13,125 ft) or more.

Petroleum and natural gas are pumped from beneath the ocean floor using huge offshore drilling rigs. Almost a quarter of the world's petroleum and natural gas now comes from under the ocean.

Another useful resource, salt, is dissolved in the sea water itself. Since ancient times people have used the process of evaporation to remove salt from sea water. Much of the world's salt is still obtained using this natural process.

There is still another valuable ocean resource—water. In some parts of the world, freshwater supplies are so limited that water is taken from the ocean. The salt is removed from sea water by **desalination**. In one method, sea water is evaporated, leaving the minerals behind. The water vapor is then cooled and condensed back into fresh water. In another desalination method, sea water is passed through a plastic film that allows pure water, but not the dissolved salts, to go through.

✔ **What resources do people take from the ocean?**

Offshore drilling rigs like this one may stand in water as deep as 300 m (about 1000 ft). ►

▲ Desalination plants like this one provide water for drinking or industry. Right now the cost is usually too high to use desalinated water for farm irrigation.

Summary

Ocean exploration has a long history. Today's ocean scientists have a wide range of technology that they can use, including scuba equipment, submersibles, satellites, and sonar. The oceans also contain valuable natural resources such as fish, petroleum, minerals, and sea water itself.

Review

1. What did the crew of the *Challenger* study?
2. Why are submersibles such as *Alvin* valuable to ocean scientists?
3. What mineral resources are found in or beneath the ocean?
4. **Critical Thinking** The deeper you go in the ocean, the greater the water pressure. Use logical reasoning to **infer** why.
5. **Test Prep** Which word does NOT belong with the others?
   A seaweed
   B salt
   C manganese
   D iron

LINKS

MATH LINK

Calculate A typical dive with *Alvin* lasts about 9 hours. Of these 9 hours, 30 minutes are spent launching the craft. Another 30 minutes are spent recovering it from the water. The descent to the ocean floor takes $2\frac{1}{2}$ hours, and the ascent back to the surface takes another $2\frac{1}{2}$ hours. How long do the scientists have for research?

WRITING LINK

Narrative Writing—Story Choose an ocean resource to research. Find out more about this resource, including how it is obtained and how it is used. Then write a science fiction story for your class that describes a world where that resource has become scarce.

LITERATURE LINK

***Exploring the* Titanic** The complete story of the *Titanic* expedition is told in this book by Robert D. Ballard. In 1985 Ballard and his team discovered the remains of the *Titanic* on the ocean floor. A year later the team returned to explore the ship in the submersible *Alvin*.

TECHNOLOGY LINK

Learn more about ocean exploration by viewing *Jacques Cousteau* on the **Harcourt Science Newsroom Video.**

CNN Turner Le@rning

Saltwater Agriculture

Who would grow crops in a desert? Scientists would, and they are using saltwater to do it.

By the Sea

The first major use of salt water for growing crops was in Israel. At the end of World War II, Hugo and Elisabeth Boyko decided to live there. Elisabeth was a horticulturist, an expert in growing certain plants, and Hugo was an ecologist.

The Boykos used their skills to landscape a town near the Red Sea. They wanted to make it prettier so that more people would move there. Growing plants in the seaside town was a challenge. Most plants need rich soil and fresh water to grow, but here the land was sandy and the only water was from the sea. They pumped salt water from the sea to irrigate, or water, their plants. Many plants are killed by salt water, but the Boykos noticed that some plants survived in spite of the salt.

Since then other scientists have continued the Boykos' work. Some have teamed up with desert farmers in Mexico, India, and

This photograph shows a landscaped town along the Red Sea.

Glasswort is a halophyte. It can grow in salty soil.

other countries to build experimental farms that practice saltwater agriculture.

A Growing Challenge

Why grow crops in a desert? And why use salty seawater instead of fresh water from rivers or lakes? There are some very important reasons.

The world's population is increasing, so there are more and more people to feed. But Earth's supplies of good farmland and fresh water are shrinking. Every year it gets harder to raise enough food for everyone. Where could farmers find additional land and water? Areas of desert near an ocean seem like an excellent choice.

Saltwater Crops

Corn, wheat, rice, potatoes, and soybeans are the main crops that people eat. Salt water kills them all. What else is there? Halophytes. Halophytes are plants that grow in the wild and survive in salty soil. In fact, halophytes absorb salt and store it inside themselves. That's why some of them taste so salty.

One halophyte that could be used for food is called glasswort. This leafless plant can be fed to livestock. Its seeds contain protein and oil, and the oil has a nutlike taste. However, glasswort isn't the perfect crop—yet. Glasswort is so salty that it makes livestock thirsty. They have to drink more water than usual which is not a good way to save fresh water, especially in a desert. Can scientists develop a less salty glasswort? Agronomists are trying.

THINK ABOUT IT

1. Why would it be useful to farm deserts near oceans?
2. What advantages and disadvantages are there to growing halophytes?

WEB LINK:
For science and technology updates, visit The Learning Site. www.harcourtschool.com

Careers Hydrologist

What They Do Hydrologists test drinking water, issue flood warnings, check underground water supplies, and protect water in other ways. Many work in government agencies, city or state offices, consulting firms, and waste-treatment plants.

Education and Training A person wishing to become a hydrologist needs to study physical or natural science or engineering and take courses in soils, marine biology, or other scientific fields. Math and computer skills are also helpful.

PEOPLE IN SCIENCE

Robert D. Ballard

UNDERSEA EXPLORER

"Captain Nemo in Twenty Thousand Leagues Under the Sea by Jules Verne is who I always wanted to be. Absolutely no doubt about it."

Undersea explorer Robert D. Ballard made headlines around the world when he and his crew located the wreck of the R.M.S. *Titanic*. Although most people know of Dr. Ballard for making this discovery, his fellow scientists know him for discovering deep-ocean life forms and geologic processes never seen before.

Although geologists had hypothesized that thermal vents existed, no one had predicted that there would be so many kinds of organisms there. Dr. Ballard observed huge blood-red worms without eyes or mouths, clusters of giant clams, blind crabs, and other strange animals. These animals depend on bacteria, not on plants, for food.

Inside the submersible *Alvin*

Dr. Ballard's team is also recognized for discovering that all the water of the oceans is recycled over time through Earth's crust. This discovery has helped scientists explain why sea water is full of minerals.

Interested in becoming an undersea explorer from the time he was a boy, Dr. Ballard is thankful to the many people who taught and encouraged him throughout his career. "You need to pick out certain people you have great respect for and listen to them," he says. "At every critical point in my life, when I was ready to quit, I can point to someone who said, 'Keep it up.'"

THINK ABOUT IT

1. Why was discovering that all the water of the oceans is recycled through Earth's crust important?
2. Why is working as part of a team important to scientists?

Water World

What happens when waters meet?

Materials

- water
- 200-mL beaker
- food coloring
- hot plate
- tongs
- water-filled aquarium

Procedure

1. Fill the beaker half-full of water. Add food coloring to the water.

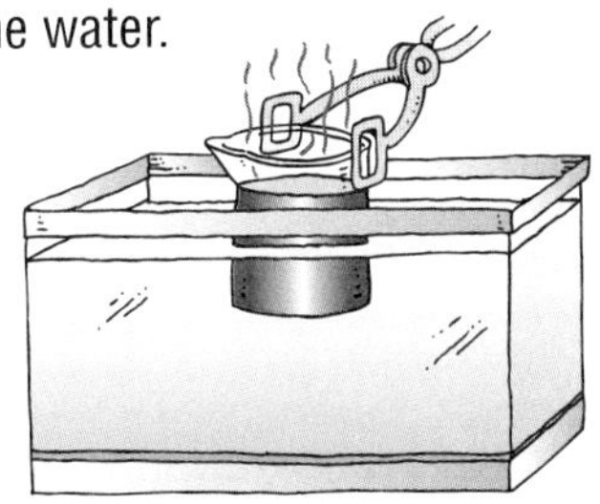

2. Using the hot plate, gently warm the water in the beaker.
3. Your teacher or another adult will use the tongs to lower the beaker straight down into the aquarium filled with cold water.
4. Observe the hot, colored water as it leaves the beaker.

Draw Conclusions

Describe what you observed. From your observations, what conclusions can you draw about areas in the ocean where warm currents flow through cooler waters?

Oil and Water

Why did ancient sailors use oil to calm the seas near their ships?

Materials

- glass bread pan
- water
- food coloring
- drinking straw
- cooking oil

Procedure

1. Fill the glass pan about half-full of water.

2. Add several drops of food coloring to the water.
3. Using the straw, gently blow across the surface of the water.
4. Now slowly pour oil into the water until it forms a layer of oil about 1 cm thick on top of the water.
5. Using the straw, blow gently across the surface again.

Draw Conclusions

Compare the waves produced in Step 3 with those produced in Step 5. What do you conclude to be the cause of any differences in the waves? Why would sailors pour oil on the water during rough weather?

Chapter 4 Review and Test Preparation

Vocabulary Review

Use the terms below to complete the sentences. The page numbers in ( ) tell you where to look in the chapter if you need help.

wave (C94)
current (C96)
tide (C98)
estuary (C102)
shore (C102)
tide pool (C103)
headland (C103)
jetty (C104)
scuba (C109)
submersible (C109)
sonar (C109)
desalination (C112)

1. The ____, which is the repeated rise and fall in the level of the ocean, is caused by the pull of gravity of the moon and the sun.

2. The area where the ocean and the land meet and interact is the ____.

3. Scientists can use self-contained underwater breathing apparatus, or ____, equipment to dive beneath the water.

4. In an ocean ____, a stream of water moves through the ocean like a river, but in a ____, water moves up and down in a circular motion.

5. A ____ is a small underwater vehicle used to explore the ocean.

6. A body of water at the mouth of a river is an ____.

7. Scientists can use ____ to map the ocean floor.

8. A pool of sea water found along a rocky shore is called a ____.

9. A ____ is a rocky point that juts out into the ocean.

10. A ____ is a wall-like structure made of rocks that sticks out into the ocean.

11. The process of ____ removes the salt from sea water.

Connect Concepts

Use terms from the Word Bank to complete the concept map below.

wave **tide** **submersible**
scuba **shore**

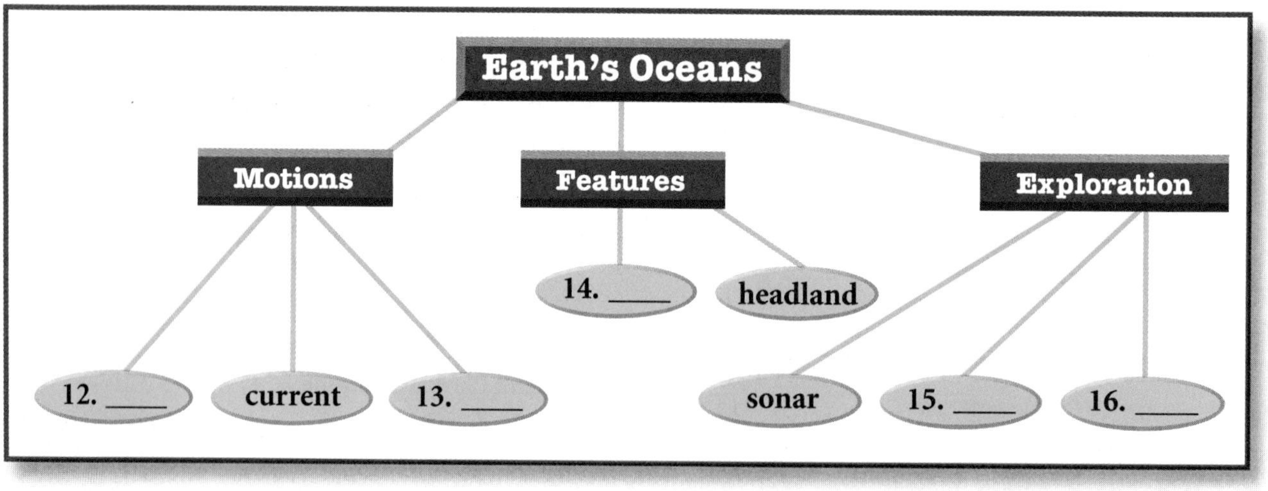

Check Understanding

Write the letter of the best choice.

17. A tsunami is a wave caused by —
    A an earthquake C a storm surge
    B a high tide D an ocean current

18. The main cause of tides is —
    F ocean waves
    G the moon's gravity
    H the sun's energy
    J longshore currents

19. Deep-ocean currents are caused by —
    A volcanoes deep under water
    B prevailing winds
    C the Earth's rotation
    D differences in water temperature

20. Shoreline currents are caused by —
    F local winds and conditions
    G prevailing winds
    H the saltiness of the water
    J sandspits

21. Most erosion at the shore is caused by —
    A currents C waves
    B deposition D tides

22. Detailed study of the oceans began with —
    F the discovery of the *Titanic*
    G the invention of scuba gear
    H the voyage of the *Challenger*
    J the scientists of the *Trieste*

23. Scientists explore the oceans with —
    A satellites C sonar
    B scuba D all of the above

24. *Alvin* is a ____ that scientists used to discover hot springs deep under the ocean.
    F sailboat H satellite
    G submersible J robot

Critical Thinking

25. Suppose you drop a ball into the ocean in a place where there is no current. Will waves move the ball quickly away, or will it bob in place? Explain.

26. Suppose you have the choice of buying one of two houses. Both houses are built near the beach. One is 50 m from the ocean. The other is 100 m from the ocean. Which house would you choose? Explain.

27. Suppose you are an ocean miner. Tell how you might obtain a mineral that is on the ocean bottom, 1000 m below the surface.

Process Skills Review

28. How can you **make a model** of a tide pool?

29. Which method of **measuring** works better to determine the depth of the ocean—sonar or weighted ropes? Explain.

Performance Assessment

Waves

Using construction paper, glue, and two pieces of string, make a model to compare the way *energy* in waves travels with the way *water* in waves travels.

Unit Project Wrap Up

Here are some ideas for ways to wrap up your unit project.

Graph Earthquakes

Research the magnitude of the last five earthquakes reported in the United States. Make a graph to show your data. You can use a computer and graphing software to make your graph.

Invent Weather Instruments

Design instruments that will help you measure weather conditions. Write directions that will help others use your instruments.

Make a Map

Investigate the route of an explorer who traveled on an ocean. Make a map to show the explorer's route.

Investigate Further

How could you make your project better? What other questions do you have about Earth's surface? Plan ways to find answers to your questions. Use the Science Handbook on pages R2-R9 for help.

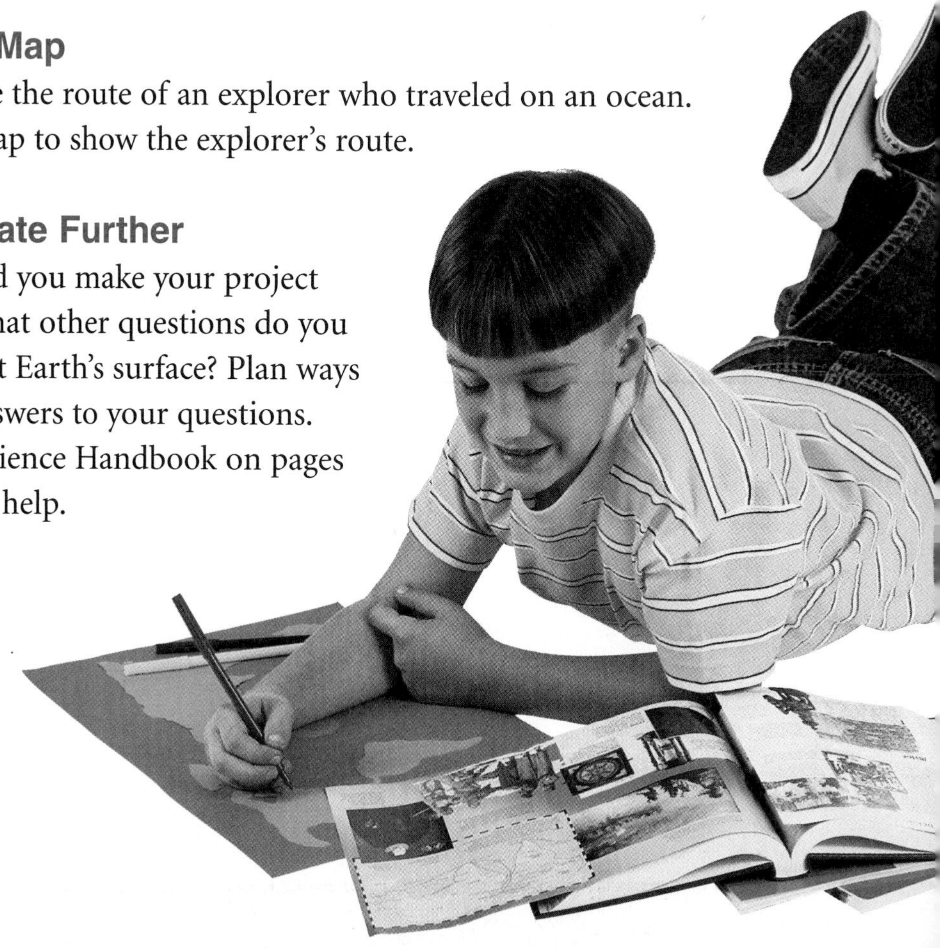

References

Planning an Investigation

When scientists observe something they want to study, they use the method of scientific inquiry to plan and conduct their study. They use science process skills as tools to help them gather, organize, analyze, and present their information. This plan will help you use scientific inquiry and process skills to work like a scientist.

Step 1—Observe and ask questions.

I wonder which design of paper airplane will fly the greatest distance?

- Use your senses to make observations.
- Record a question you would like to answer.

Step 2—Make a hypothesis.

My hypothesis: This airplane with the narrow wings will fly the greatest distance.

- Choose one possible answer, or hypothesis, to your question.
- Write your hypothesis in a complete sentence.
- Think about what investigation you can do to test your answer.

Step 3—Plan your test.

I'll launch each airplane three times from the same spot, with the same amount of force.

- Write down the steps you will follow to do your test. Decide how to conduct a fair test by controlling variables.
- Decide what equipment you will need.
- Decide how you will gather and record your data.

I'll record each distance, then find the average distance each airplane traveled.

Step 4—Conduct your test.

- Follow the steps you wrote.
- Observe and measure carefully.
- Record everything that happens.
- Organize your data so that you can study it carefully.

My hypothesis was correct. The airplane with the narrow wings flew the greatest distance.

Step 5—Draw conclusions and share results.

- Analyze the data you gathered.
- Make charts, graphs, or tables to show your data.
- Write a conclusion. Describe the evidence you used to determine whether your test supported your hypothesis.
- Decide whether your hypothesis was true.

Investigate Further

I wonder which airplane will fly for the longest time?

Using Science Tools

Using a Hand Lens

A hand lens magnifies objects, or makes them look larger than they are.

1. Hold the hand lens about 12 centimeters (5 in.) from your eye.
2. Bring the object toward you until it comes into focus.

Using a Thermometer

A thermometer measures the temperature of air and most liquids.

1. Place the thermometer in the liquid. Don't touch the thermometer any more than you need to. Never stir the liquid with the thermometer. If you are measuring the temperature of the air, make sure that the thermometer is not in line with a direct light source.
2. Move so that your eyes are even with the liquid in the thermometer.
3. If you are measuring a material that is not being heated or cooled, wait about two minutes for the reading to become stable. Find the scale line that meets the top of the liquid in the thermometer, and read the temperature.
4. If the material you are measuring is being heated or cooled, you will not be able to wait before taking your measurements. Measure as quickly as you can.

Caring for and Using a Microscope

A microscope is another tool that magnifies objects. A microscope can increase the detail you see by increasing the number of times an object is magnified.

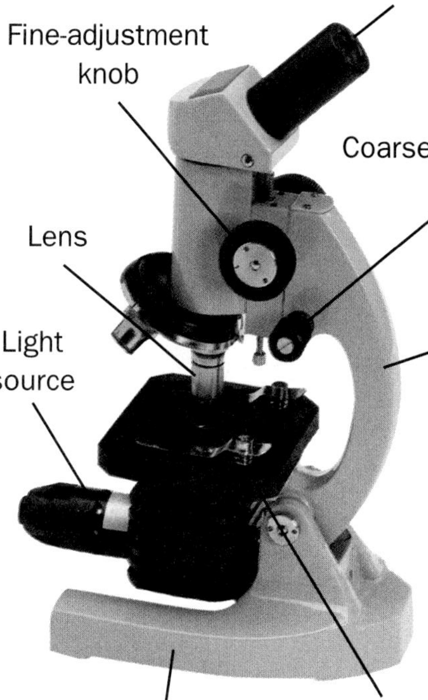

A Light Microscope

Caring for a Microscope

- Always use two hands when you carry a microscope.
- Never touch any of the lenses of a microscope with your fingers.

Using a Microscope

1. Raise the eyepiece as far as you can using the coarse-adjustment knob. Place your slide on the stage.
2. Always start by using the lowest power. The lowest-power lens is usually the shortest. Start with the lens in the lowest position it can go without touching the slide.
3. Look through the eyepiece, and begin adjusting it upward with the coarse-adjustment knob. When the slide is close to being in focus, use the fine-adjustment knob.
4. When you want to use a higher-power lens, first focus the slide under low power. Then, watching carefully to make sure that the lens will not hit the slide, turn the higher-power lens into place. Use only the fine-adjustment knob when looking through the higher-power lens.

You may use a Brock microscope. This is a sturdy microscope that has only one lens.

1. Place the object to be viewed on the stage.
2. Look through the eyepiece, and begin raising the tube until the object comes into focus.

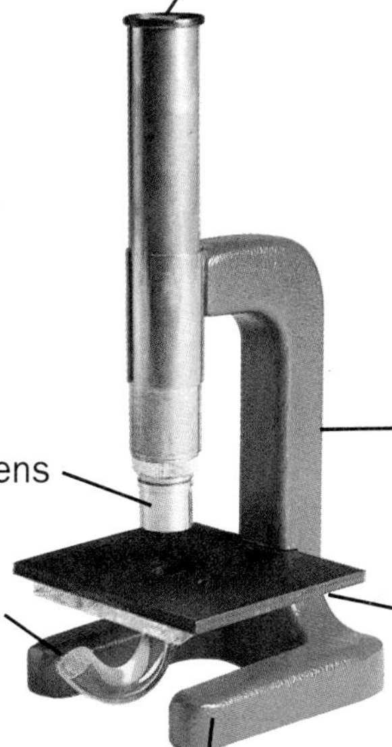

A Brock Microscope

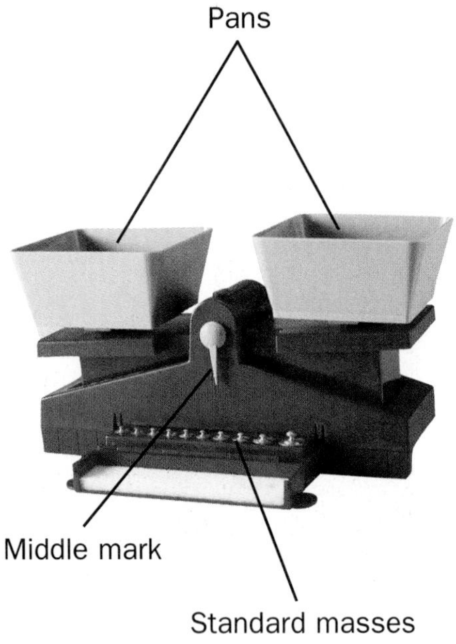

Using a Balance

Use a balance to measure an object's mass. Mass is the amount of matter an object has.

1. Look at the pointer on the base to make sure the empty pans are balanced.
2. Place the object you wish to measure in the left pan.
3. Add the standard masses to the other pan. As you add masses, you should see the pointer move. When the pointer is at the middle mark, the pans are balanced.
4. Add the numbers on the masses you used. The total is the mass in grams of the object you measured.

Using a Spring Scale

Use a spring scale to measure forces such as the pull of gravity on objects. You measure weight and other forces in units called newtons (N).

Measuring the Weight of an Object

1. Hook the spring scale to the object.
2. Lift the scale and object with a smooth motion. Do not jerk them upward.
3. Wait until any motion of the spring comes to a stop. Then read the number of newtons from the scale.

Measuring the Force to Move an Object

1. With the object resting on a table, hook the spring scale to it.
2. Pull the object smoothly across the table. Do not jerk the object.
3. As you pull, read the number of newtons you are using to pull the object.

Beaker **Graduate**

Measuring Liquids

Use a beaker, a measuring cup, or a graduate to measure liquids accurately.

1. Pour the liquid you want to measure into a measuring container. Put your measuring container on a flat surface, with the measuring scale facing you.
2. Look at the liquid through the container. Move so that your eyes are even with the surface of the liquid in the container.
3. To read the volume of the liquid, find the scale line that is even with the surface of the liquid.
4. If the surface of the liquid is not exactly even with a line, estimate the volume of the liquid. Decide which line the liquid is closer to, and use that number.

Using a Ruler or Meterstick

Use a ruler or meterstick to measure distances and to find lengths of objects.

1. Place the zero mark or end of the ruler or meterstick next to one end of the distance or object you want to measure.
2. On the ruler or meterstick, find the place next to the other end of the distance or object.
3. Look at the scale on the ruler or meterstick. This will show the distance you want or the length of the object.

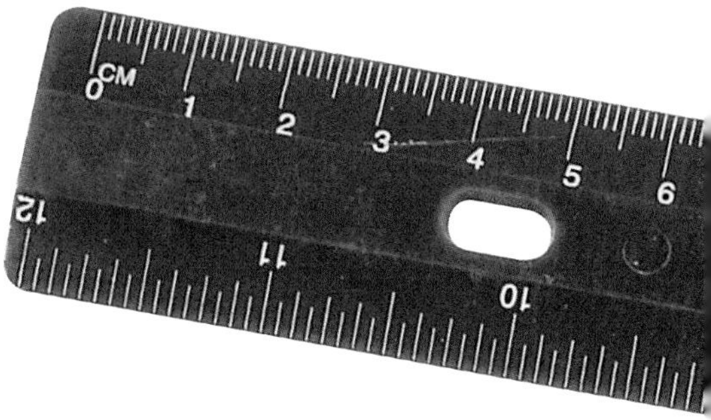

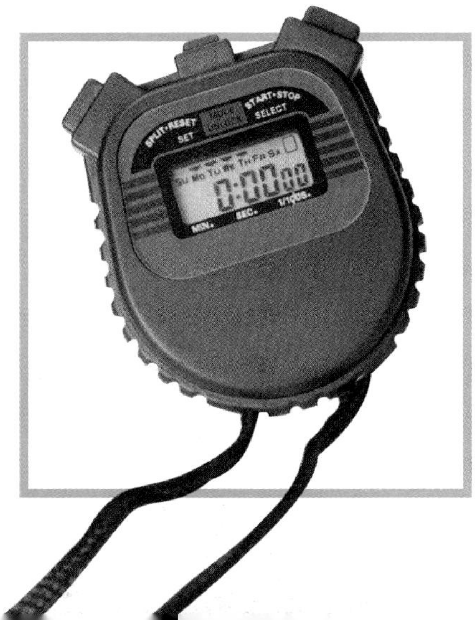

Using a Timing Device

Use a timing device such as a stopwatch to measure time.

1. Reset the stopwatch to zero.
2. When you are ready to begin timing, press start.
3. As soon as you are ready to stop timing, press stop.
4. The numbers on the dial or display show how many minutes, seconds, and parts of seconds have passed.

Using a Computer

A computer can help you communicate with others and can help you get information. It is a tool you can use to write reports, make graphs and charts, and do research.

Writing Reports

To write a report with a computer, use a word processing software program. After you are in the program, type your report. By using certain keys and the mouse, you can control how the words look, move words, delete or add words and copy them, check your spelling, and print your report.

Save your work to the desktop or hard disk of the computer, or to a floppy disk. You can go back to your saved work later if you want to revise it.

There are many reasons for revising your work. You may find new information to add or mistakes you want to correct. You may want to change the way you report your information because of who will read it. Computers make revising easy. You delete what you don't want, add the new parts, and then save. You can save different versions of your work if you want to.

For a science lab report, it is important to show the same kinds of information each time. With a computer, you can make a general format for a lab report, save the format, and then use it again and again.

Making Graphs and Charts

You can make a graph or chart with most word processing software programs. Or, you can use special software programs such as Data ToolKit or Graph Links. With Graph Links you can make pictographs and circle, bar, line, and double-line graphs.

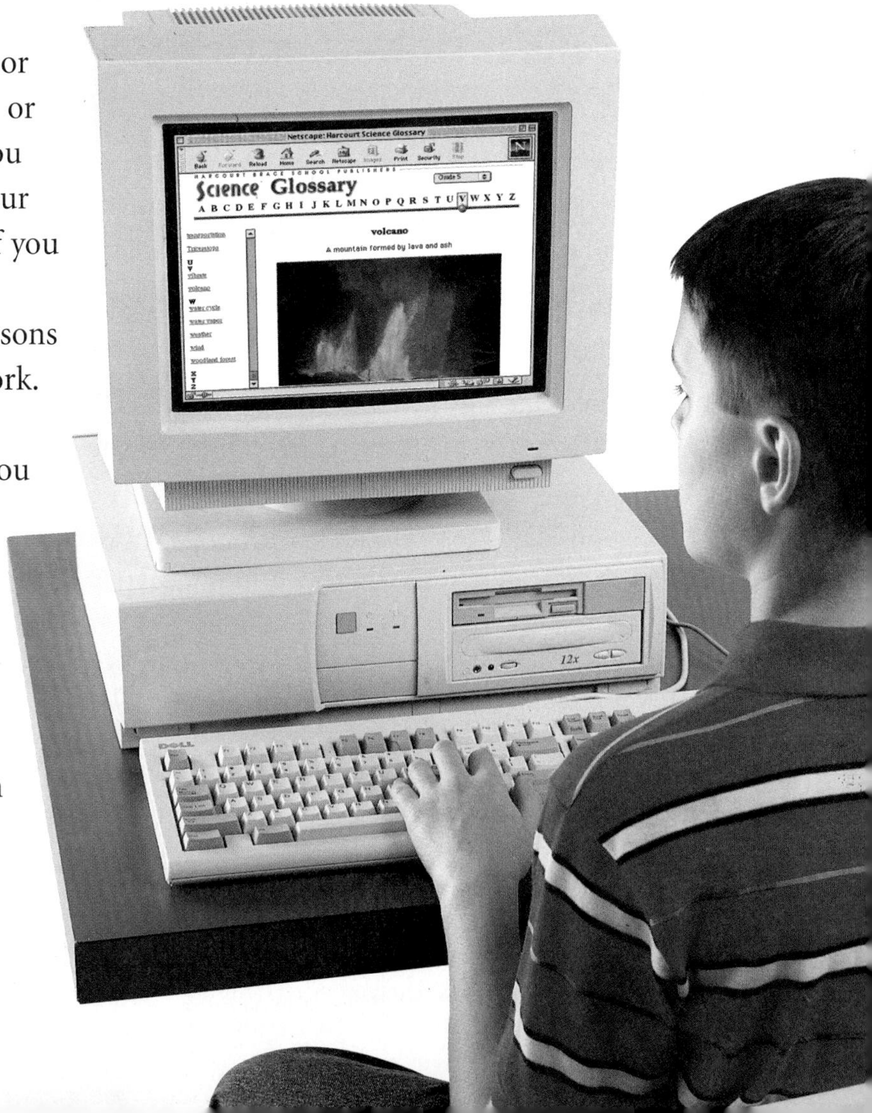

First, decide what kind of graph or chart will best communicate your data. Sometimes it's easiest to do this by sketching your ideas on paper. Then you can decide what format and categories you need for your graph or chart. Choose that format for the program. Then type your information. Most software programs include a tutor that gives you step-by-step directions for making a graph or chart.

Doing Research

Computers can help you find current information from all over the world through the Internet. The Internet connects thousands of computer sites that have been set up by schools, libraries, museums, and many other organizations.

Get permission from an adult before you log on to the Internet. Find out the rules for Internet use at school or at home. Then log on and go to a search engine, which will help you find what you need. Type in keywords, words that tell the subject of your search. If you get too much information that isn't exactly about the topic, make your keywords more specific. When you find the information you need, save it or print it.

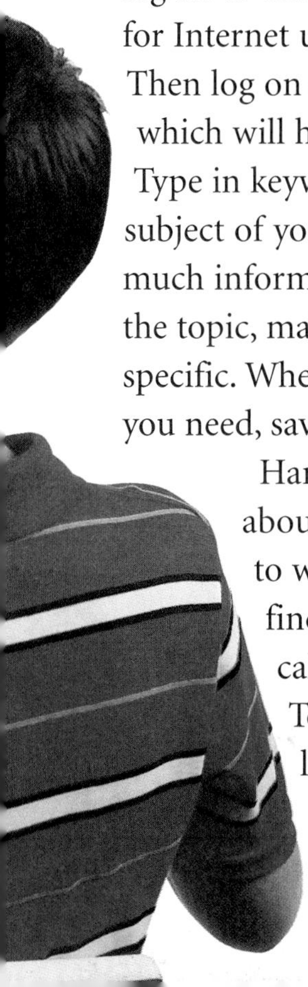

Harcourt Science tells you about many Internet sites related to what you are studying. To find out about these sites, called Web sites, look for Technology Links in the lessons in this book.

If you need to contact other people to help in your research, you can use e-mail. Log into your e-mail program, type the address of the person you want to reach, type your message, and send it. Be sure to have adult permission before sending or receiving e-mail.

Another way to use a computer for research is to access CD-ROMs. These are discs that look like music CDs. CD-ROMs can hold huge amounts of data, including words, still pictures, audio, and video. Encyclopedias, dictionaries, almanacs, and other sources of information are available on CD-ROMs. These computer discs are valuable resources for your research.

Visit the Multimedia Science Glossary to see illustrations of these words and to hear them pronounced.
www.harcourtschool.com/scienceglossary

Glossary

This Glossary contains important science words and their definitions. Each word is respelled as it would be in a dictionary. When you see the ′ mark after a syllable, pronounce that syllable with more force than the other syllables. The page number at the end of the definition tells where to find the word in your book. The boldfaced letters in the examples in the Pronunciation Key that follows show how these letters are pronounced in the respellings after each glossary word.

PRONUNCIATION KEY

a	**a**dd, m**a**p	m	**m**ove, see**m**	u	**u**p, d**o**ne
ā	**a**ce, r**a**te	n	**n**ice, ti**n**	û(r)	b**ur**n, t**er**m
â(r)	c**are**, **air**	ng	ri**ng**, so**ng**	yo͞o	f**u**se, f**ew**
ä	p**a**lm, f**a**ther	o	**o**dd, h**o**t	v	**v**ain, e**v**e
b	**b**at, ru**b**	ō	**o**pen, s**o**	w	**w**in, a**w**ay
ch	**ch**eck, cat**ch**	ô	**o**rder, j**aw**	y	**y**et, **y**earn
d	**d**og, ro**d**	oi	**oi**l, b**oy**	z	**z**est, mu**s**e
e	**e**nd, p**e**t	ou	p**ou**t, n**ow**	zh	vi**si**on, plea**s**ure
ē	**e**qual, tr**ee**	o͝o	t**oo**k, f**u**ll	ə	the schwa, an unstressed vowel representing the sound spelled
f	**f**it, hal**f**	o͞o	p**oo**l, f**oo**d		*a* in **a***bove*
g	**g**o, lo**g**	p	**p**it, sto**p**		*e* in *sick***e***n*
h	**h**ope, **h**ate	r	**r**un, poo**r**		*i* in *poss***i***ble*
i	**i**t, g**i**ve	s	**s**ee, pa**ss**		*o* in *mel***o***n*
ī	**i**ce, wr**i**te	sh	**s**ure, ru**sh**		*u* in *circ***u***s*
j	**j**oy, le**dg**e	t	**t**alk, si**t**		
k	**c**ool, ta**k**e	th	**th**in, bo**th**		
l	**l**ook, ru**l**e	th̶	**th**is, ba**th**e		

Other symbols:
- • separates words into syllables
- ′ indicates heavier stress on a syllable
- ′ indicates light stress on a syllable

A

acceleration [ak•sel′ər•ā′shən] A change in motion caused by unbalanced forces or a change in velocity **(F13, F35)**

acid rain [as′id rān′] Precipitation resulting from pollution condensing into clouds and falling to Earth **(B99)**

action force [ak′shən fôrs′] The first force in the third law of motion **(F43)**

air pressure [âr′ presh′ər] The weight of air **(C65)**

alveoli [al•vē′ə•lē] Tiny air sacs located at the ends of bronchi in the lungs **(A18)**

angiosperm [an′jē•ō•spûrm′] A flowering plant **(A77)**

anthracite [an′thrə•sīt′] A hard, black rock; the fourth stage of coal formation **(C45)**

asexual reproduction [ā•sek′shōō•əl rē′prə•duk′shən] Reproduction by simple cell division **(A41)**

atmosphere [at′məs•fir] The layer of air that surrounds Earth **(C64)**

atom [at′əm] The smallest unit of an element that has all the properties of that element **(E40)**

axis [ak′sis] An imaginary line that passes through Earth's center and its North and South Poles **(D7)**

B

balanced forces [bal′ənst fôrs′əz] The forces acting on an object that are equal in size and opposite in direction, canceling each other out **(F12)**

biomass [bī′ō•mas′] Organic matter, such as wood, that is living or was recently alive **(F110)**

biome [bī′ōm′] A large-scale ecosystem **(B64)**

bitumen [bi•tōō′mən] A fairly hard, dark brown or black rock; the third stage of coal formation **(C45)**

bone marrow [bōn′ mar′ō] A connective tissue that produces red and white blood cells **(A24)**

C

capillaries [kap′ə•ler′ēz] The smallest blood vessels **(A17)**

carbon dioxide–oxygen cycle [kär′bən dī•ok′sīd′ ok′sə•jən sī′kəl] The process by which carbon and oxygen cycle among plants, animals, and the environment **(B8)**

cell [sel] The basic unit of structure and function of all living things **(A6)**

cell membrane [sel′ mem′brān′] The thin covering that encloses a cell and holds its parts together **(A8)**

cellular respiration [sel′yōō•lər res′pə•rā′shən] The process by which cells release the energy in food to carry on life processes **(A100)**

chemical bonds [kem′i•kəl bondz′] The forces that join atoms to each other **(F98)**

chlorophyll [klôr′ə•fil′] A pigment, or coloring matter, that helps plants use light energy to produce sugars **(A70)**

chromosome [krō′mə•sōm′] A threadlike strand inside the nucleus that is made up of DNA **(A39)**

climate [klī′mit] The average of all weather conditions through all seasons over a period of time **(C78)**

climate zone [klī′mit zōn′] A region throughout which yearly patterns of temperature, rainfall, and amount of sunlight are similar **(B64)**

climax community [klī′maks′ kə•myōō′nə•tē] The last stage of succession **(B93)**

combustibility [kəm•bus′tə•bil′ə•tē] The chemical property of being able to burn **(E24)**

community [kə•myōō′nə•tē] All the populations of organisms living together in an environment **(B28)**

competition [kom′pə•tish′ən] The contest among organisms for the limited resources of an ecosystem **(B42)**

compound [kom′pound] A substance made of the atoms of two or more different elements **(E48)**

condensation [kon′dən•sā′shən] The process by which a gas changes back into a liquid **(B14, C67, E17)**

conduction [kən•duk′shən] The direct transfer of heat between objects that touch **(F85)**

conductor [kən•duk′tər] A material that conducts electrons easily **(F70)**

conserving [kən•sûrv′ing] The saving or protecting of resources **(B104)**

consumer [kən•sōō′mər] An organism in a community that must eat to get the energy it needs **(B34)**

continental drift [kon′tə•nen′təl drift′] A theory of how Earth's continents move over its surface **(C22)**

convection [kən•vek′shən] The transfer of heat as a result of the mixing of a liquid or a gas **(F85)**

core [kôr] The center of the Earth **(C15)**

corona [kə•rō′nə] The sun's atmosphere **(D33)**

cotyledons [kot′ə•lēd′ənz] The structures where food is stored in seeds **(A116)**

crust [krust] The thin, outer layer of Earth **(C14)**

current [kur′ənt] A stream of water that flows like a river through the ocean **(C96)**

cytoplasm [sīt′ō•plaz′əm] A jellylike substance containing many chemicals that keep a cell functioning **(A9)**

D

decomposer [dē′kəm•pōz′ər] Consumer that breaks down the tissues of dead organisms **(B35)**

density [den′sə•tē] The concentration of matter in an object **(E9)**

deposition [dep′ə•zish′ən] The process of dropping, or depositing, sediment in a new location **(C7)**

desalination [dē•sal′ə•nā′shən] The process of removing salt from sea water **(C112)**

diffusion [di•fyōō′zhən] The process by which many materials move in and out of cells **(A10)**

direct development [də•rekt′ di•vel′əp•mənt] A kind of growth where organisms keep the same body features as they grow larger **(A46)**

dominant trait [dom′ə•nənt trāt′] A strong trait **(A53)**

E

earthquake [ûrth′ kwāk′] A shaking of the ground caused by the sudden release of energy in Earth's crust **(C18)**

eclipse [i•klips′] The passing of one object through the shadow of another **(D8)**

ecosystem [ek′ō•sis′təm] A community and its physical environment together **(B28)**

electric charge [i•lek′trik chärj′] The charge obtained by an object when it gains or loses electrons **(F68)**

electric circuit [i•lek′trik sûr′kit] The path along which electrons can flow **(F71)**

electric current [i•lek′trik kûr′ənt] The flow of electrons from negatively charged objects to positively charged objects **(F69)**

electric force [i•lek′trik fôrs′] The attraction or repulsion of objects due to their charges **(F69)**

electromagnet [i•lek′trō•mag′nit] A temporary magnet made by passing electric current through a wire coiled around an iron bar **(F72)**

electron [ē•lek′tron′] A subatomic particle with a negative charge **(E39)**

element [el′ə•mənt] A substance made up of only one kind of atom **(E40)**

El Niño [el nēn′yō] A short-term climate change that occurs every two to ten years **(C81)**

embryo [em′brē•ō] The tiny plant inside a seed **(A116)**

endangered [en•dān′jərd] A term describing a population of organisms that is likely to become extinct if steps are not taken to save it **(B51)**

energy [en′ər•jē] The ability to cause changes in matter **(F62)**

energy pyramid [en′ər•jē pir′ə•mid] Shows the amount of energy available to pass from one level of a food chain to the next **(B38)**

epidermis [ep′ə•dûr′mis] The outer layer of cells of a leaf **(A96)**

erosion [i•rō′zhən] The process of moving sediment from one place to another **(C7)**

estuary [es′chōō•er′ē] The place where a freshwater river empties into an ocean **(B80, C102)**

evaporation [ē•vap′ə•rā′shən] The process by which a liquid changes into a gas **(B14, C67, E16)**

exotic [ik•sä′•tic] An imported or nonnative organism. **(B50)**

extinct [ik•stingkt′] No longer in existence; describes a species when the last individual of a population dies and that organism is gone forever **(B51)**

F

fault [fôlt] A break or place where pieces of Earth's crust move **(C18)**

fertilization [fûr′təl•ə•zā′shən] The joining of a male reproductive cell with a female reproductive cell **(A110)**

fiber [fī′bər] Any material that can be separated into threads **(A84)**

food chain [fōōd′ chān′] The ways in which the organisms in an ecosystem interact with one another according to what they eat **(B35)**

food web [fōōd′ web′] Shows the interactions among many different food chains in a single ecosystem **(B36)**

force [fôrs] A push or pull that causes an object to move, stop, or change direction **(F6)**

fossil [fos′əl] The remains or traces of past life found in sedimentary rock **(C23)**

fossil fuel [fos′əl fyōō′əl] A fuel formed from the remains of once-living organisms **(C42)**

friction [frik′shən] A force that opposes, or acts against, motion when two surfaces rub against each other **(F6)**

fusion energy [fyo͞o′zhən en′ər•jē] The energy released when the nuclei of two atoms are forced together to form a larger nucleus **(F112)**

G

galaxy [gal′ək•sē] A group of stars, gas, and dust **(D46)**

gas [gas] The state of matter that does not have a definite shape or volume **(E14)**

gene [jēn] Structures on a chromosome that contain the DNA code for a trait an organism inherits **(A54)**

geothermal energy [jē′ō•thûr′məl en′ər•jē] Heat from inside the Earth **(F111)**

germinate [jûr′mə•nāt′] To sprout as a seed does **(A118)**

global warming [glō′bəl wôrm′ing] The hypothesized rise in Earth's average temperature from excess carbon dioxide **(C82)**

grafting [graft′ing] A form of artificial reproduction that can produce desirable characteristics in woody plants **(A120)**

grain [grān] The seed of certain plants **(A82)**

gravitation [grav′i•tā′shən] The force that pulls all objects in the universe toward one another **(F8)**

gravitropism [grav′i•trō′piz•əm] A plant's response to gravity **(A105)**

greenhouse effect [grēn′hous′ i•fekt′] process by which the Earth's atmosphere absorbs heat **(C82)**

gymnosperm [jim′nə•spûrm′] Plant with unprotected seeds; conifer or cone-bearing plant **(A76)**

H

habitat [hab′ə•tat′] A place in an ecosystem where a population lives **(B29)**

headland [hed′land′] A hard, rocky point of land left when softer rock is washed away by the sea **(C103)**

heat [hēt] The transfer of thermal energy from one substance to another **(F84)**

humidity [hyo͞o•mid′ə•tē] A measure of the amount of water in the air **(C65)**

hydroelectric energy [hī′drō•ē•lek′trik en′ər•jē] Electricity generated from the force of moving water **(F104)**

I

individual [in′də•vij′o͞o•əl] A single organism in an environment **(B28)**

inertia [in•ûr′shə] The property of matter that keeps it moving in a straight line or keeps it at rest **(F41)**

inherited trait [in•her′it•əd trāt′] A characteristic that is passed from parent to offspring **(A52)**

instinct [in′stingkt] A behavior that an organism inherits **(B46)**

insulator [in′sə•lāt′ər] A material that does not carry electrons **(F71)**

intertidal zone [in′tər•tīd′əl zōn′] An area where the tide and churning waves provide a constant supply of oxygen and nutrients to living organisms **(B77)**

J

jetty [jet′ē] A wall-like structure made of rocks that sticks out into the ocean **(C104)**

joint [joint] A place where bones meet and are attached to each other and to muscles **(A24)**

K

kinetic energy [ki•net′ik en′ər•jē] The energy of motion, or energy in use **(F62)**

L

landform [land′fôrm′] A physical feature on Earth's surface **(C6)**

law of universal gravitation [lô′ uv yōōn′ə•vûr′səl grav′i•tā′shən] Law that states that all objects in the universe are attracted to all other objects **(F49)**

learned behavior [lûrnd′ bē•hāv′yər] A behavior an animal learns from its parents **(B46)**

lens [lenz] A piece of clear material that bends, or refracts, light rays passing through it **(F77)**

life cycle [līf′ sī′kəl] The series of distinct stages of life that most organisms grow and mature through **(A46)**

ligament [lig′ə•mənt] One of the bands of connective tissue that hold a skeleton together **(A25)**

light-year [līt′yir′] The distance light travels in one Earth year; about 9.5 trillion km **(D47)**

lignite [lig′nīt′] A soft, brown rock; the second stage of coal formation **(C44)**

liquid [lik′wid] The state of matter that has a definite volume but no definite shape **(E14)**

local winds [lō′kəl windz′] The winds dependent upon local changes in temperature **(C73)**

M

machine [mə•shēn′] Something that makes work easier by changing the size or the direction of a force **(F20)**

magma [mag′mə] A hot, soft rock from Earth's lower mantle **(C16)**

magnetism [mag′nə•tiz′əm] The force of repulsion (pushing) or attraction (pulling) between poles of magnets **(F7)**

magnitude [mag′nə•tōōd] Brightness of stars **(D38)**

main sequence [mān′ sē′kwəns] A band of stars that includes most stars of average color, size, magnitude, and temperature **(D39)**

mantle [man′təl] The layer of rock beneath Earth's crust **(C14)**

mass [mas] The amount of matter in an object **(E7)**

mass movement [mas′ mōōv′mənt] The downhill movement of rock and soil because of gravity **(C9)**

matter [mat′ər] Anything that has mass and takes up space **(E6)**

meiosis [mī•ō′sis] The process that reduces the number of chromosomes in reproductive cells **(A42)**

metamorphosis [met′ə•môr′fə•sis] A change in the shape or characteristics of an organism's body as it grows **(A47)**

microclimate [mī′krō•klī′mit] The climate of a very small area **(C78)**

mitosis [mī•tō′sis] The process of cell division **(A39)**

molecule [mol′ə•kyōōl′] A grouping of two or more atoms joined together **(E40)**

momentum [mō•men′təm] A measure of how hard it is to slow down or stop an object **(F36)**

N

natural gas [nach′ər•əl gas′] A gas, methane, usually found with petroleum **(C43)**

natural resource [nach′ər•əl rē′sôrs′] Any of the useful minerals and other materials that people take from the Earth **(C36)**

near-shore zone [nir′shôr′ zōn′] The area beyond the breaking waves that extends to waters that are about 180 m deep **(B77)**

nephrons [nef′ronz′] Tubes inside the kidneys where urea and water diffuse from the blood **(A20)**

net force [net′ fôrs′] The result of two or more forces acting together on an object **(F14)**

neuron [nŏŏr′on′] A specialized cell that can receive information and transmit it to other cells **(A26)**

neutron [nōō′tron′] A subatomic particle with no charge **(E39)**

niche [nich] The role each population has in its habitat **(B29)**

nitrogen cycle [nī′trə•jən sī′kəl] The cycle in which nitrogen gas is changed into forms of nitrogen that plants can use **(B7)**

nonrenewable resource [non′ri•nōō′ə•bəl rē′sôrs′] A resource that cannot be readily replaced once it is used **(C36)**

nonvascular [non•vas′kyə•lər] Not having xylem and phloem; said of some plants **(A74)**

nuclear energy [nōō′klē•ər en′ər•jē] The energy released when the nucleus of an atom is split apart **(F110)**

nucleus [nōō′klē•əs] **1** *(cell)* The organelle that controls all of a cell's activities. **2** *(atom)* The center of an atom. **(A8, E39)**

O

open-ocean zone [ō′pən•ō′shən zōn′] The area that includes most deep ocean waters; most organisms live near the surface **(B77)**

orbit [ôr′bit] The path one body in space takes as it revolves around another body; such as that of Earth as it revolves around the sun **(D7, F48)**

organ [ôr′gən] Tissues that work together to perform a specific function **(A12)**

osmosis [os•mō′sis] The diffusion of water and dissolved materials through cell membranes **(A10)**

ovary [ō′və•rē] The portion of a flower, at the base of the pistil, that contains the eggs **(A111)**

P

palisade layer [pal′ə•sād′ lā′ər] The layer of cells in a leaf where most photosynthesis occurs **(A97)**

Pangea [pan•jē′ə] A supercontinent containing all of Earth's land that existed about 225 million years ago **(C22)**

peat [pēt] A soft, brown material made up of partly decayed plants; first stage of coal formation **(C44)**

periodic table [pir′ē•od′ik tā′bəl] The table of elements in order of increasing atomic number; grouped by similar properties **(E47)**

phloem [flō′em] The tubes that transport food in the vascular plants **(A69)**

photosphere [fōt′ə•sfir′] The visible surface of the sun **(D33)**

photosynthesis [fōt′ō•sin′thə•sis] The process by which plants make food **(A96)**

phototropism [fō•tō•trō′piz•əm] A plant's response to light **(A104)**

physical properties [fiz′i•kəl prop′ər•tēz] The characteristics of a substance that can be observed or measured without changing the substance **(E6)**

pioneer plants [pī′ə•nir′ plantz′] The first plants to invade a bare area **(B92)**

pistil [pis′təl] The female part of a flower **(A110)**

pitch [pich] An element of sound determined by the speed which sound waves move **(F79)**

plate [plāt] The rigid blocks of crust and upper mantle rock **(C15)**

pollen [pol′ən] Flower structures that contain the male reproductive cells **(A76)**

pollution [pə•lo͞o′shən] Waste products that damage an ecosystem **(B99)**

population [pop•yə•lā′shən] All the individuals of the same kind living in the same environment **(B28)**

position [pə•zish′ən] An object's place, or location **(F34)**

potential energy [pō•ten′shəl en′ər•jē] The energy an object has because of its place or its condition **(F62)**

power [pou′ər] The amount of work done for each unit of time **(F19)**

precipitation [pri•sip′ə•tā′shən] Any form of water that falls from clouds, such as rain or snow **(B14, C65)**

prevailing winds [prē•vāl′ing windz′] The global winds that blow constantly from the same direction **(C73)**

producer [prə•do͞os′ər] An organism that makes its own food **(B34)**

proton [prō′ton′] A subatomic particle with a positive charge **(E39)**

R

radiation [rā′dē•ā′shən] The transfer of thermal energy by electromagnetic waves **(F85)**

reaction force [rē•ak′shən fôrs′] The force that pushes or pulls back in the third law of motion **(F43)**

reactivity [rē′ak•tiv′ə•tē] The ability of a substance to go through a chemical change **(E23)**

receptors [ri•sep′tarz] Nerve cells that detect conditions in the body's environment **(A26)**

recessive trait [ri•ses′iv trāt′] A weak trait **(A53)**

reclamation [rek′lə•mā′shən] The process of restoring a damaged ecosystem **(B110)**

recycle [rē•sī′kəl] To recover a resource from an item and use the recovered resource to make a new item **(B105)**

recycling [rē•sī′kling] The process of taking a resource from a product and making it into a new product **(C52)**

reduce [ri•do͞os′] To cut down on the use of resources **(B104)**

reflection [ri•flek′shən] The light energy that bounces off objects **(F76)**

refraction [ri•frak′shən] The bending of light rays when they pass through a substance **(F76)**

renewable resource [ri•no͞o′ə•bəl rē′sôrs] A resource that is replaced as it is used **(C38)**

resistor [ri•zis′tər] A material that resists the flow of electrons in some way **(F71)**

reusable resource [rē•yo͞o′zə•bəl rē′sôrs] A natural resource that is renewed by natural cycles and can be used more than once; an inexhaustible resource **(C38)**

reuse [ri′yo͞oz′] To use items again; sometimes for a different purpose **(B105)**

revolve [ri•volv′] To travel in a closed path around an object such as Earth does as it moves around the sun **(D6)**

rotate [rō′tāt] The spinning of Earth on its axis **(D7)**

S

satellite [sat′ə•līt′] A natural body, like the moon, or an artificial object that orbits another object **(D15)**

scuba [sko͞o′bə] Underwater breathing equipment; the letters stand for **s**elf-**c**ontained **u**nderwater **b**reathing **a**pparatus **(C109)**

seedling [sēd′ling] The stage when a germinated seed begins growing and making its own food **(A118)**

sexual reproduction [sek′sho͞o•əl rē′prə•duk′shən] The form of reproduction in which cells from two parents unite to form a zygote **(A42)**

shore [shôr] The area where the ocean and land meet and interact **(C102)**

solar energy [sō′lər en′ər•jē] The energy of sunlight **(F111)**

solar flare [sō′lər flâr′] A brief burst of energy from the sun's photosphere **(D34)**

solar wind [sō′lər wind′] A fast-moving stream of particles thrown into space by solar flares **(D34)**

solid [sol′id] The state of matter that has a definite shape and a definite volume **(E14)**

solubility [sol′yə•bil′ə•tē] The ability of one substance to be dissolved in another substance **(E10)**

sonar [sō′när′] A device that uses sound waves to determine water depth **(C109)**

space probe [spās′ prōb′] A robot vehicle used to explore deep space **(D16)**

speed [spēd] A measure of the distance an object moves in a given amount of time **(F35)**

spore [spôr] A single reproductive cell that grows into a new plant **(A75)**

stamen [stā′mən] The male part of a flower **(A110)**

submersible [sub•mur′sə•bəl] An underwater vehicle **(C109)**

succession [sək•sesh′ən] A gradual change in an ecosystem, sometimes occurring over hundreds of years **(B92)**

sunspot [sun′spot′] A dark spot on the photosphere of the sun **(D34)**

symbiosis [sim′bē•ō′sis] A long-term relationship between different kinds of organisms **(B45)**

system [sis′təm] Organs that work together to perform a function **(A12)**

T

telescope [tel′ə•skōp′] An instrument that magnifies distant objects, or makes them appear larger **(D15)**

temperature [tem′pər•ə•chər] The average kinetic energy of all the molecules in an object **(F84)**

tendons [ten′dənz] Tough bands of connective tissue that attach muscles to bones **(A25)**

threatened [thret′ənd] Describes a population of organisms that are likely to become endangered if they are not protected **(B51)**

tidal energy [tīd′əl en′ər•jē] A form of hydroelectric energy that produces electricity from the rising and falling of tides **(F106)**

tide [tīd] The repeated rise and fall in the level of the ocean **(C98)**

tide pool [tīd′ po͞ol′] A pool of sea water found along a rocky shoreline **(C103)**

tissue [tish′o͞o] Cells that work together to perform a specific function **(A12)**

tissue culture [tish′o͞o kul′chər] Process that grows plants artificially in laboratories **(A120)**

transpiration [tran′spə•rā′shən] The process in which plants give off water through their stomata **(B15)**

tropism [trō′piz′əm] A plant's response to a stimulus **(A104)**

U

unbalanced forces [un•bal′ənst fôrs′əz] Forces that are not equal **(F13)**

universe [yo͞on′ə•vûrs′] Everything that exists—planets, stars, dust, gases, and energy **(D46)**

V

vascular [vas′kyə•lər] Term that decribes a plant with xylem and phloem **(A74)**

vegetative propagation [vej′ə•tāt′iv prop′ə•gā′shən] A form of asexual reproduction without seeds **(A119)**

velocity [və•los′ə•tē] An object's speed in a particular direction **(F35)**

villi [vil′ī] The tiny tubes sticking into the small intestine **(A19)**

volcano [vol•kā′nō] A mountain formed by lava and ash **(C16)**

volume [vol′yo͞om] **1** *(measurement)* The amount of space that an object takes up. **2** *(sound)* The loudness of a sound **(E8, F79)**

W

water cycle [wôt′ər sī′kəl] The cycle in which Earth's water moves through the environment **(B14)**

wave [wāv] The up-and-down movement of surface water **(C94)**

weathering [weth′ər•ing] The process of breaking rock into soil, sand, and other tiny pieces **(C7)**

weight [wāt] A measure of the pull of gravity on an object **(E7)**

wetlands [wet′landz′] The water ecosystems that include saltwater marshes, mangrove swamps, and mud flats **(B111)**

work [wûrk] The use of a force to move an object through a distance **(F18)**

X

xylem [zī′ləm] The tubes that transport water and minerals in vascular plants **(A69)**

A

B

H

I

Q

R

S

T

U

V

PHOTO CREDITS:

Page Placement Key: (t)-top (c)-center (b)-bottom (l)-left (r)-right (i)-inset (bg)-background

Cover and Title Pages

Gail Shumway/FPG International; (bg) Eduardo Garcia/FPG International

Contents

Page iv Anup & Manoj Shah/Animals Animals; iv (bg) Grant V. Faint/The Image Bank; v Zig Leszczynski/Animals Animals; v (bg) Karl Hentz/The Image Bank; vi Eric & David Hosking/Photo Researchers; vi (bg) Bios (Klein-Hubert)/Peter Arnold, Inc.; vii Telegraph Colour Library/FPG International; viii Alvis Upitis/The Image Bank; viii (bg) Tim Crosby/Liaison International; ix David Zaitz/Photonica; ix (bg) Tony Stone Images

Unit A

Unit Opener Insert, Anup & Manoj Shah/Animals Animals; (bg) Grant V. Faint/The Image Bank; A1 (c) Anup & Manoj Shah/Animals Animals; A1 (l) Grant V. Faint/The Image Bank; A2-A3 Image Shop/Phototake; A3 (l) Lawrence Migdale/Photo Researchers; A3 (c) Quest/Science Photo Library/Photo Researchers; A4 Charles D. Winters/Timeframe Photography, Inc./Photo Researchers; A6 (l) The Granger Collection, New York; A6 (c), (r) Courtesy of Hunt Institute for Botanical Documentation, Carnegie Mellon University, Pittsburgh, PA; A7 (tr) Michel Viard/Peter Arnold, Inc.; A7 (bl) Courtesy of Dr. Sam Harbo D.V.M., and Dr. Jurgen Schumacher D.V.M., Veterinary Hospital, University of Tennessee; A7 (br) A.B. Sheldon/Dembinsky Photo Associates; A7 (tl) Ed Reschke/Peter Arnold, Inc.; A8 Dwight R. Kuhn; A9 Courtesy of Dr. Sam Harbo D.V.M., and Dr. Jurgen Schumacher D.V.M., Veterinary Hospital, University of Tennessee; A10 Biophoto Associates/Science Source/Photo Researchers; A11 (l) J. Barry O'Rourke/The Stock Market; A11 (r) Jim Brown/The Stock Market; A14 Michael Newman/PhotoEdit; A16 (l) Dr. Tony Brain/Science Photo Library/Photo Researchers; A16 (r) Prof. P. Motta/Dept. of Anatomy/University "La Sapienza", Rome/Science Photo Library/Photo Researchers; A22 Gary Holscher/Tony Stone Images; A28 (l) Kevin Collins/Visuals Unlimited; A28 (r) Alferd Pasieka/Peter Arnold, Inc.; A29 (l) Barbara Wright/Animlas Animals; A29 (r) Dr. Dennis Kunkel/Phototake; A30 NASA; A33 Charles D. Winters/Timeframe Photography, Inc./Photo Researchers; A34-A35 Rob & Ann Simpson/Visuals Unlimited; A35 (l) Dr. D. Spector/Peter Arnold, Inc.; A35 (r) Dwight R. Kuhn; A36 Ron Kimball; A38 (l) Jerome Wexler/Photo Researchers; A38 (r) Kenneth H. Thomas/Photo Researchers; A38 (c) Carolina Biological Supply Company/Phototake; A38 (cl) Carolina Biological Supply Company/Phototake; A38 (cr) Jerome Wexler/Photo Researchers; A39 Conly L. Rieder/BPS/Tony Stone Images; A40 (c) Noble Proctor/Photo Researchers; A40 (b) Zig Leszczynski/Animals Animals; A40 (tl), (tc), (tr) Carolina Biological Supply Company/Phototake; A41 (b) Bob Gossington/Bruce Coleman, Inc.; A41 (tl), (tc), (tr), A43 Carolina Biological Supply Company/Phototake; A44 J.H. Robinson/Photo Researchers; A46 (t) Peter A. Simon/Phototake; A46 (b) Dr. E.R. Degginger/Photo Researchers; A47 (l) Thomas Gulz/Visuals Unlimited; A47 (r) William J. Weber/Visuals Unlimited; A47 (c) Dwight R. Kuhn; A48 Harry Rogers/Photo Researchers; A49 Michael Fogden/Bruce Coleman, Inc.; A50 Paul Barton/The Stock Market; A52 Phil Savoie/The Picture Cube; A53 The Granger Collection, New York; A56 Tim Davis/Tony Stone Images; A57 (t) College of Veterinary Medicine/University of Florida; A57 (b) Zigy Kaluzny/Tony Stone Images; A58 (t) Henry Friedman/HRW; A58 (b) Oliver Meckes/Photo Researchers; A62-A63 Tom Bean/Tony Stone Images; A63 (t) Inga Spence/Visuals Unlimited; A63 (b) Ned Therrien/Visuals Unlimited; A64 James Randklev/Tony Stone Images; A66 (l) Matt Meadows/Peter Arnold, Inc.; A66 (r) Reinhard Siegel/Tony Stone Images; A66 (c) Richard Choy/Peter Arnold, Inc.; A67 (bl) Dr. E.R. Degginger, FPSA/Color-Pic; A67 (br) John Kaprielian/Photo Researchers; A67 (t) Norman Myers/Bruce Coleman, Inc.; A69 Jane Grushow/Grant Heilman Photography; A70-A71 (t) Runk/Schoenberger/Grant Heilman Photography; A70 (b) Alan Levenson/Tony Stone Images; A70 (ti) Runk/Schoenberger/Grant Heilman Photography; A72 Darrell Gulin/Dembinsky Photo Associates; A74 Kim Taylor/Bruce Coleman, Inc.; A75 Runk/Schoenberger/Grant Heilman Photography; A76 (t) Runk/Schoenberger/Grant Heilman Photography; A76 (b) S.J. Krasemann/Peter Arnold, Inc.; A77 (t) Dr. E.R. Degginger/Color-Pic; A77 (b) Robert Maier/Earth Scenes; A78 (animal life cycle) (t) Gregory K. Scott/Photo Researchers; A78 (r) Harry Rogers/National Audubon Society/Photo Researchers; A78 (b) David M. Dennis/Tom Stack & Associates; A78 (l) Jen & Des Bartlett/Bruce Coleman, Inc.; A78 (plant life cycle) (t) Dr. E.R. Degginger/Color-Pic; A78 (r) Barry L. Runk/Grant Heilman Photography; A78 (b) Jane Grushow/Grant Heilman Photography; A78 (l) Dwight R. Kuhn; A84 (l) Alan & Linda Detrick/Photo Researchers; A84 (r) Angelina Lax/Photo Researchers; A85 Grant Heilman/Grant Heilman Photography; A85 (i) Will & Deni McIntyre/Photo Researchers; A86 D. Cavagnaro/DRK; A87 (t) Dr. Dennis Kunkel/Phototake; A87 (b) Mark Richards/PhotoEdit; A88 Special Collections, California Academy of Science; A90 (l) Runk/Schoenberger/Grant Heilman Photography; A90 (r) Dr. E.R. Degginger/Color-Pic; A91 James Randklev/Tony Stone Images; A92-A93 Tony Craddock/Tony Stone Images; A93 (t) R. & E. Thane/Earth Scenes; A93 (b) Nuridsany et Perennou/Photo Researchers; A94 Steven Ogilvy/Picture It/Harcourt; A96 Wendell Metzen/Bruce Coleman, Inc.; A98 Dr. Kenneth R. Miller/Science Photo Library/Photo Researchers; A99 Dr. E.R. Degginger/Color-Pic; A100 B.W. Hoffmann/AGStock USA; A100 (i) Bachmann/Photo Researchers; A102 Peter Steiner/The Stock Market; A104 Cathlyn Melloan/Tony Stone Images; A105 (l) Runk/Schoenberger/Grant Heilman Photography; A105 (r) Lee Rentz/Bruce Coleman, Inc.; A106 (t) Michael Hubrich/Dembinsky Photo Associates; A106 (c) John Shaw/Bruce Coleman, Inc.; A106 (b) Phyllis A. Betow/Bruce Coleman, Inc.; A108 Gay Bumgarner/Tony Stone Images; A110 (l) Leonard Lee Rue, III/Photo Researchers; A110 (r) Dwight R. Kuhn; A110 (tli) Dick Scott/Dembinsky Photo Associates; A110 (ri) Dr. E.R. Degginger/Color-Pic; A110 (bli) Michael P. Gadomski/Photo Researchers; A112 (l) Pal Hermansen/Tony Stone Images; A112 (r) Hans Pfletschinger/Peter Arnold, Inc.; A113 Merlin Tuttle/Photo Researchers; A114 Frans Lanting/Minden Pictures; A117 (t) David Cavagnaro/Peter Arnold, Inc.; A117 (b) Kevin Schafer Photography; A117 (tc) Dr. E. R. Degginger/Bruce Coleman, Inc.; A117 (bc) Gregory K. Scott/Photo Researchers; A117 (bg) Jeff Lepore/Photo Researchers; A118 Runk/Schoenberger/Grant Heilman Photography; A119 (tl) Kenneth W. Fink/Photo Researchers; A119 (tr) Jerome Wexler/National Audubon Society/Photo Researchers; A119 (b) G.I. Bernard/Earth Scenes; A120 (l) Dr. E.R. Degginger/Color-Pic; A120 (r) Rosenfeld Images, Ltd./Science Photo Library/Photo Researchers; A120-A121 (t) G. R. Roberts Photo Library; A121 (i) Holt Studios, Int./Photo Researchers; A122 Dana Downie/AGStock USA; A123 (b) Mark Richards/PhotoEdit; A124 Dennis Carlyle Darling/HRW; A126 Wendy W. Cortesi; A127 Gay Bumgarner/Tony Stone Images; A128 (l) Grant V. Faint/The Image Bank; A128 (i) Anup & Manoj Shah/Animals Animals

Unit B

Unit Opener Insert, Zig Leszczynski/Animals Animals; (bg) Karl Hentz/The Image Bank; B1 (c) Zig Leszczynski/Animals Animals; B1 (l) Karl Hentz/The Image Bank; B2-B3 Superstock; B3 (t) Clyde H. Smith/Peter Arnold, Inc.; B3 (b) Earl Roberge/Photo Researchers; B4 Wolfgang Kaehler Photography; B6 Randy Ury/The Stock Market; B7 Thomas Hovland/Grant Heilman Photography; B10 Wolfgang Kaehler Photography; B12 Michael Giannechini/Photo Researchers; B14-B15 Greg Vaughn/Tony Stone Images; B16 (t) C. Vincent/Natural Selection Stock Photography; B16 (b) Bob Daemmrich Photography, Inc.; B16 (bi) Superstock; B18-B19 Lee Rentz/Bruce Coleman, Inc.; B19 (t) John Shaw/Bruce Coleman, Inc.; B19 (b) Ken Graham/Bruce Coleman, Inc.; B20 (t) Sipa Press; B20 (b) Jeff Foott/Bruce Coleman, Inc.; B22 Greg Vaughn/Tony Stone Images; B23 C. Vincent/Natural Selection Stock Photography; B24-B25 P & R Hagan/Bruce Coleman, Inc.; B25 (l) Mitsuaki Iwago/Minden Pictures; B25 (r) Tomas del Amo/Pacific Stock; B26 Tim Davis/Photo Researchers; B28-B29 (bg) J.A. Kravlis/Masterfile; B28 (l) Michael Giannechini/Photo Researchers; B28-B29 (i) Ted Kerasote/Photo Researchers; B29 (b) Mitsuaki Iwago/Minden Pictures; B29 (t) Superstock; B30 (tl) David Muench Photography, Inc.; B30 (tr), (bl) Barry L. Runk/Grant Heilman Photography; B30 (br) David Muench Photography, Inc.; B32 Superstock; B34-B35 (bg) Larry Ditto/Bruce Coleman, Inc.; B34 (tl) V.P. Weinland/Photo Researchers; B34 (tr) Parviz M. Pour/Photo Researchers; B34-B35 (b) Dembinsky Photo Associates; B35 (l) Tom McHugh/Photo Researchers; B35 (r) Tom & Pat Leeson/Photo Researchers; B36-B37 Woods, Michael J./NGS Image Collection; B39 Bruce Coleman, Inc.; B40 Joe McDonald/McDonald Wildlife Photography; B42 (l) Roger Bickel/New England Stock Photo; B42 (bg) Stuart Westmorland/Tony Stone Images; B42 (r) Bruce Coleman, Inc.; B43 (l) Kevin Schafer/Peter Arnold, Inc.; B43 (r) Mitsuaki Iwago/Minden Pictures; B44 (t) John Shaw/Bruce Coleman, Inc.; B44 (c) Hal H. Harrison/Photo Researchers; B44 (b) Wayne Lankinen/Bruce Coleman, Inc.; B45 (t) M. & C. Photography/Peter Arnold, Inc.; B45 (b) William Townsend/Photo Researchers; B46 (t) Vince Streano/The Stock Market; B46-B47 (b) Ralph Ginzburg/Peter Arnold, Inc.; B48 Bryan & Cherry Alexander/Masterfile; B50 (t) Tim Davis/Photo Researchers; B50 (bl) Johnny Johnson/Tony Stone Images; B50 (br) Malcolm Boulton/Photo Researchers; B51 Tom McHugh/Photo Researchers; B52 (b) Roy Toft/Tom Stack & Associates; B52-B53 (t) Galen Rowell/Mountain Light; B54 Gunter Ziesler/Peter Arnold, Inc.; B55 (t) Doug Cheeseman/Peter Arnold; B55 (b) Bonnie Kamin/PhotoEdit; B56 (t) Louisiana State University Chemistry Library Website; B56 (b) Meckes/Ottawa/Photo Researchers; B60-B61 Craig Tuttle/The Stock Market; B61 (l) Earth Satellite Corporation/Science Photo Library/Photo Researchers; B61 (r) Jake Rajs/Tony Stone Images; B62 Chromosohm/Sohm/Tony Stone Images; B64 (t) David Muench Photography; B64 (b) Gary Braasch/Tony Stone Images; B65 (tl) Superstock; B65 (tr) Steve Kaufman/Peter Arnold, Inc.; B65 (br) Colin Prior/Tony Stone Images; B65 (bl) Joseph Van Os/The Image Bank; B66 Wolfgang Kaehler Photography; B66 (i) Mark Moffett/Minden Pictures; B67 Superstock; B67 (i) Roger Bickel/New England Stock Photo; B68 David Muench Photography; B68 (i) William Manning/The Stock Market; B69 (i) T. Eggers/The Stock Market; B69 Darrell Gulin/Tony Stone Images; B70 David Muench Photography, Inc.; B70 (i) Joseph Van Os/The Image Bank; B71 (b) Carr Clifton/Minden Pictures; B71 (t) Kennan Ward; B72 (l) Nicholas DeVore, III/Bruce Coleman, Inc.; B72 (r) Tui De Roy/Minden Pictures; B74 Stan Osolinski/The Stock Market; B80 (b) David Muench Photography, Inc.; B80 (t) Jim Brandenburg/Minden Pictures; B82 NASA GSFC/Science Photo Library/Photo Researchers; B83 (t) Manfred Kage/Peter Arnold; B83 (b) Pete Saloutos/The Stock Market; B84 (t) Romberg Tiburon Center; B84 (b) Emory Kristof/NGS Image Collection; B86 Jim Bradenburg/Minden Pictures; B88-B89 Gary Brettnacher/Tony Stone Images; B89 (t) Jonathan Wallen; B89 (b) Argus Fotoarchiv/Peter Arnold, Inc.; B90 Frans Lanting/Minden Pictures; B92 Runk/Schoenberger/Grant Heilman Photography; B93 (t) Kennan Ward; B93 (b) Ed Reschke/Peter Arnold, Inc.; B94 (t) Larry Nielsen/Peter Arnold, Inc.; B94 (c) John Marshall/Tony Stone Images; B94 (b) Jeff & Alexa Henry/Peter Arnold, Inc.; B96 Art Wolfe/Tony Stone Images; B98 (i) Dr. E.R. Degginger/Color-Pic; B98 Mark E. Gibson; B99 J.H. Robinson/Photo Researchers; B100 Francois Gohier/Photo Researchers; B101 Tony Arruza/Bruce Coleman, Inc.; B104 (c) Jim Corwin/Tony Stone Images; B106 Tim Davis/Photo Researchers; B110 Mark E. Gibson; B111 (l) Bernard Boutrit/Woodfin Camp & Associates; B111 (r) Bill Tiernan/The Virginian-Pilot; B112 (i) Key Sanders/Tony Stone Images; B112 Wolfgang Kaehler Photography; B114 (tl) Superstock; B114 (tr) Tom Bean/The Stock Market; B115 John Hyde/Bruce Coleman, Inc.; B116 (t) Centre For Ecological Studies; B116 (b) E. Hanumantha/Photo Researchers; B120 (l) Karl Hentz/The Image Bank; B120 (i) Zig Leszczynski/Animals Animals

Unit C

Unit Opener Insert, Eric & David Hosking/Photo Researchers; (bg) Bios (Klein-Hubert)/Peter Arnold, Inc.; C1 (c) Eric & David Hosking/Photo Researchers; C1 (l) Bios (Klein-Hubert)/Peter Arnold, Inc.; C2-C3 Roger Werth/Woodfin Camp & Associates; C3 (t) John Livzey/Tony Stone Images; C3 (b) Royal Oservatory, Edinburgh/Science Photo Library/Photo Researchers; C4 Tom Bean/Tom & Susan Bean, Inc.; C6-C7 (b) Eric Neurath/Stock, Boston; C6 (bi) Mark E. Gibson; C6 (tr) Tom Bean/Tom & Susan Bean, Inc.; C6 (tl) Helen Paraskevas; C7 NASA Photo/Grant Heilman Photography; C8 Mark E. Gibson; C9 M.T. O'Keefe/Bruce Coleman, Inc.; C10-C11 Michael Collier/Stock, Boston; C12 Soames Summerhays/Photo Researchers; C16 G. Gualco/Bruce Coleman, Inc.; C17 (t) Gregory G. Dimijian/Photo Researchers; C17 (c) Krafft/Explorer/Science Source/Photo Researchers; C17 (b) Tom & Pat Leeson/Photo Researchers; C18 UPI-Bettmann/Corbis; C20 M.P.L. Fogden/Bruce Coleman, Inc.; C23 Tom Bean/Tom & Susan Bean, Inc.; C24 (t), (b) The Natural History Museum, London; C24 (ct) Martin Land/Science Photo Library/Photo Researchers; C24 (cb) A. Kerstitch/Bruce Coleman, Inc.; C25 R.T. Nowitz/Photo Researchers; C26 Walter H. F. Smith & David T. Sandwell/NOAA National Data Centers; C27 (t) NASA; C27 (b) David Young-Wolff/PhotoEdit; C28 (t) Santa Fabio/Black Star/Harcourt; C28 (b) Tom Bean/Tom & Susan Bean, Inc.; C31 (l) Dr. E.R. Degginger/Color-Pic; C3l (r) Joyce Photographics/Photo Researchers; C32-C33 Terry Vine/Tony Stone Images; C33 (t) Bruce Hands/Tony Stone Images; C33 (b) Joe Sohm/Chromosohm/Stock, Boston; C34 (t) Arnold Fisher/Science Photo Library/Photo Researchers; C34 (b) Runk/Schoenberger/Grant Heilman Photography; C36 Dr. E.R. Degginger/Color-Pic; C36-C37 Debra P. Hershkowitz/Bruce Coleman, Inc.; C37 (c), (b), (tl), (tr) Dr. E.R. Degginger/Color-Pic; C37 (tc) Vanessa Vick/Photo Researchers; C38-C39 Michael P. Gadomski/Photo Researchers; C40 J.C. Carton/Bruce Coleman, Inc.; C42 (l) Larry Lefever/Grant Heilman Photography; C42 (r) Thomas Kitchin/Tom Stack & Associates; C43 Kenneth Murray/Photo Researchers; C44 (l) Dr. E.R. Degginger/Color-Pic; C44 (r), C45 (l) Breck P. Kent/Earth Scenes; C45 (r) Dr. E.R. Degginger, FPSA/Color-Pic; C48 Richard B. Levine; C50 Matt Meadows/Peter Arnold, Inc.; C51 Jack W. Dykinga/Bruce Coleman, Inc.; C51 (i) David Aronson/Stock, Boston; C52 (bg) Dick Rowen/Photo Researchers; C52 (t) Henneghien/Bruce Coleman, Inc.; C52 (cr) Michele Burgess/Stock, Boston; C54 Shell Photo Service; C55 (t) Jeremy Hardie/Tony Stone Images; C55 (b) David R. Frazier; C56 (t) Otis Imbodenngs/NGS Image Collection; C56 (b) AP Photo/Damian Dovarganes/Wide World Photos; C59 David Young-Wolff/Tony Stone Images; C60-C61 Bob Abraham/The Stock Market; C61 (t) NASA/The Stock Market; C61 (b) Stan Osolinski/The Stock Market; C62 Warren Faidley/International Stock Photography; C64 (l) Everett Johnson/Tony Stone Images; C64 (r) Warren Faidley/International Stock Photography; C65 (bg) Orion/International Stock Photography; C65 (bli) M. Antman/The Image Works; C65 (bri) Dr. E. R. Degginger/Color-Pic; C66 (t) David M. Grossman/Photo Researchers; C66 (b) Mark Stephenson/Corbis; C68 (l) Dan Sudia/Photo Researchers; C68 (tr) Kent Wood/Photo Researchers; C68 (br) Gary Meszaros/Dembinsky Photo Associates; C68 (cr) Kevin Schafer/Peter Arnold, Inc.; C76 Richard Brown/Tony Stone Images; C78 (l) Tom Till; C78 (r) Coco McCoy/Rainbow; C78 (c) Blaine Harrington III/The Stock Market; C79 (t) Randy Ury/The Stock Market; C79 (c) Larry Cameron/Photo Researchers; C79 (b) Jeff Greenberg/Photo Researchers; C80 (l) Ron Sefton/Bruce Coleman, Inc.; C80 (r) Jose Fuste Raga/The Stock Market; C80 (c) John Lawrence/Tony Stone Images; C80 (cl) Fritz Prenzel/Peter Arnold, Inc.; C80 (cr) Marcello Bertinetti/Photo Researchers; C81 Paul Sequeira/Photo Researchers; C81 (i) Joe Sohm/Chromosomm/Photo Researchers; C82-C83 J. Richardson/Corbis; C84 Brad Gaber/The Stock Market; C85 (bg) A. Ramey/Woodfin Camp & Associates; C85 (tr) Phil Degginger/Bruce Coleman, Inc.; C85 (bl) NASA; C86 (t) Eli Reichman/HRW; C86 (b) NASA/Goddard Space Flight Center/Science Photo Library/Photo Researchers; C90-C91 RKO Radio Pictures/Archive Photos; C91 (t) Thomas Abercrombiengs/NGS Image Collection; C91 (b) Clyde H. Smith/Peter Arnold, Inc.; C92 George D. Lepp/Photo Researchers; C94 Vince Cavataio/Pacific Stock; C95 (t) The Stock Market; C95 (bl) UPI-Bettmann/Corbis; C95 (ti) Michael P. Gadomski/Bruce Coleman, Inc.; C95 (br) Chip Porter/AllStock/PNI; C96 (b) Dr. Richard Legeckis/Science Photo Library/Photo Researchers; C96 (t) Tony Arruza/Bruce Coleman, Inc.; C97 George Marler/Bruce Coleman, Inc.; C98 John Elk/Stock, Boston; C102 (l) Brian Parker/Tom Stack & Associates; C102 (r) S.L. Craig, Jr./Bruce Coleman, Inc.; C103 (l) William E. Ferguson; C103 (r) Tom & Susan Bean, Inc.; C104 (t) Bruce Roberts/Photo Researchers; C104 (c) William Johnson/Stock, Boston; C104-C105 (b) Bob Daemmrich/Stock, Boston; C104 (bi) Wendel Metzer/Bruce Coleman, Inc.; C106 Michael Paris Photography; C108 (bl) Corbis; C108 (br), (t) The Granger Collection, New York; C108-C109 (bg) Eric Le Norcy-Bios/Peter Arnold, Inc.; C109 (tl) Naval Undersea Museum; C109 (tr) NASA/Science Photo Library/Photo Researchers; C109 (br) James P. Blair/NGS Image Collection; C109 (bl) Courtesy Smithsonian Diving Office/Photograph by Diane L. Nordeck; C110 (t) Woods Hole Oceanographic Institution; C110 (bl), (br), C111 (t) Emory Kristof/NGS Image Collection; C111 (c) Culver Pictures; C111 (b) Woods Hole Oceanographic Institution; C112 Allen Green/Photo Researchers; C113 Christian Vioujard/Liaison Agency Inc.; C114 Eric Freedman/Bruce Coleman, Inc.; C115 (t) Mike Price/Bruce Coleman, Inc.; C115 (b) David Woodfall/Tony Stone Images; C116 (t) Susan Lapides/Woodfin Camp & Associates; C116 (b) Emory Kristof/NGS Image Collection; C120 (l) Bios (Klein-Hubert)/Peter Arnold, Inc.; C120 (i) Eric & David Hosking/Photo Researchers

Unit D

Unit Opener Insert, D1 Telegraph Colour Library/FPG International; D2-D3 Guodo Cozzi/Bruce Coleman, Inc.; D3 (l) Ray Pfortner/Peter Arnold, Inc.; D3 (r) Painting by Helmut Wimmer; D4 NASA; D6, D7 Frank Rossotto/StockTrek; D8 (t) Dennis Di Cicco/Peter Arnold, Inc.; D8 (b) Frank Rossotto/StockTrek; D9, D10 (tl), (tr), (ctr), (cbr), (br) NASA; D10 (bl) Paul Stepan/Photo Researchers; D10 (ctl) Francois Gohier/Photo Researchers; D12 NASA; D14 (t), (br) The Granger Collection, New York; D14 (bl) Martha Cooper/Peter Arnold, Inc.; D14, D15, D16 (bg) Science Photo Library/Photo Researchers; D15 (tl) Sovfoto/Eastfoto; D15 (tr), (br) NASA; D15 (bl) Courtesy of AT&T Archives; D16, D17, D18-D19, D20, D21, D22, D24, D25 NASA; D26-D27 Jerry Schad/Photo Researchers; D27 (l), (r) NASA; D28 StockTrek; D31 (t) Warren Faidley/International Stock Photography; D31 (c) Pekka Parviainen/Science Photo Library/Photo Researchers; D31 (b) Brian Atkinson/Tony Stone Images; D32 (t) Rev. Ronald Royer/Science Photo Library/Photo Researchers; D32 (c) NASA; D32 (b) Hale Observatory/SS/Photo Researchers; D34 Wards Sci/Science Source/Photo Researchers; D38 John Chumack/Photo Researchers; D40 Andrea Dupree (Harvard-Smithsonian CfA), Ronald Gilliland (STScI), NASA and ESA; D41 Jeff Hester and Paul Scowen (Arizona State University), and NASA; D42 (tl) NASA; D42 (tr) Roger Ressmeyer/Corbis; D42 (b) Francois Gohier/Photo Researchers; D44 Bill Ross/Tony Stone Images; D46 Fred Espenak/Science Photo Library/Photo Researchers; D47 (b) Lynette Cook/Science Photo Library/Photo Researchers; D48 (t) Royal Observatory, Edinburgh/AATB/Science Photo Library/Photo Researchers; D48 (b) Robert Williams and the Hubble Deep Field Team (STScI) and NASA; D50 Chris Cheadle/Tony Stone Images; D51 (t) Dr. Robert Mallozzi of Universtiy of Alabama/Huntsville & NASA; D51 (b) Tony Freeman/PhotoEdit; D52 Courtesy of Julio Navarro; D56 (l), (i) Telegraph Colour Library/FPG International

Unit E

Unit Opener Insert, Alvis Upitis/The Image Bank; (bg) Tim Crosby/Liaison International; E1 (c) Alvis Upitis/The Image Bank; E1 (l) Tim Crosby/Liaison International; E2 (i) Jim Steinberg/Photo Researchers; E2-E3 Charles Krebs/The Stock Market; E3 (i) H. Armstrong Roberts, Inc.; E7 (b) NASA; E10 (b) Ron Chapple/FPG International; E10 (bi) Dr. E. R. Degginger/Color-Pic; E12 Charles D. Winters/Photo Researchers; E14 Spencer Swanger/Tom Stack & Associates; E15 (c) Phil Degginger/Color-Pic; E16 Dr. E. R. Degginger/Color-Pic; E17 Tom Pantages; E18, E19 Yoav Levy/Phototake; E20 NASA; E23 (t), (b) Tom Pantages; E23 (c) Yoav Levy/Phototake; E24 Horst Desterwinter/International Stock Photography; E25 (t) Dr. E.R. Degginger/Color-Pic; E25 (c) Norman O. Tomalin/Bruce Coleman, Inc.; E28 Joe Sohm/Photo Researchers; E29 (t) Doug Martin/Photo Researchers; E29 (b) Gary A. Conner/PhotoEdit; E30 (t) Glenn Photography; E30 (b) Geoff Tompkinson/Science Photo Library/Photo Researchers; E34-E35 Pete Saloutos/Tony Stone Images; E35 (t) Jan Taylor/Bruce Coleman, Inc.; E35 (b) Dr. E.R. Degginger/Color-Pic; E36 Superstock; E38 Lee Snider Photo Images; E40 (t) J & L Weber/Peter Arnold, Inc.; E40 (b) Dr. E.R. Degginger/Color-Pic; E41 (top to bottom) (1) Joe Towers/The Stock Market; E41 (2) Christopher S. Johnson/Stock, Boston; E41 (4) Telegraph Colour Library/FPG International; E41 (6) George Haling/Photo Researchers; E42 (li) Richard Laird/FPG International; E42 (b) Wesley Hitt/Tony Stone Images; E44 Yoav Levy/Phototake; E48 Michael Monello/Julie A. Smith Photography; E50 (l) Mel Fisher Maritime Heritage Society, Inc.; E51 Michigan Molecular Institute; E52 (t) UPI-Bettmann/Corbis; E52 (b) Mitch Kezar/Phototake; E56 (l) Tim Crosby/Liaison International; E56 (i) Alvis Upitis/The Image Bank

Unit F

Unit Opener Insert, David Zaitz/Photonica; (bg) Tony Stone Images; F1 (c) David Zaitz/Photonica; F1 (l) Tony Stone Images; F2-F3 NASA/Photo Researchers; F3 (t) NASA/ Science Photo Library/Photo Researchers; F3 (b) Jean-Loup Charmet/Science Photo Library/Photo Researchers; F6 (l) Tony Duffy/Allsport Photography; F6 (c) Pascal Rondeau/Allsport Photography; F6 (r) Allsport Photography; F7 (r) Spencer Grant/PhotoEdit; F10 David Young-Wolff/PhotoEdit; F12 (r) Mark E. Gibson; F12 (l) Myrleen Ferguson/PhotoEdit; F18 Superstock; F19 David Young-Wolff/PhotoEdit; F20 (b) Stephen Frisch/Stock, Boston; F21 (t) Novastock/PhotoEdit; F21 (ct), (b) Tony Freeman/PhotoEdit; F24, F25 NASA; F26 (t) Courtesy of Dr. Ephraim Fischbach; F26 (b) Eastern Space & Missile Center Photographic Laboratory; F30-F31 Chris Butler/Science Photo Library/Photo Researchers; F31 (t) Stephen Dalton/Photo Researchers; F31 (b) Mike Cooper/Allsport Photography; F32 E & P Bauer/Bruce Coleman, Inc.; F35 David Madison/Bruce Coleman, Inc.; F36-F37 Lee Foster/Bruce Coleman, Inc.; F36 (i) Mark E. Gibson; F38 Michael Newman/PhotoEdit; F40 (t) A.C. Cooper LTD; F40-F41 (b) Ed Degginger/Bruce Coleman, Inc.; F41 (t) NASA; F42 (t) Tony Freeman/PhotoEdit; F42 (c), (b) Larry Freeman/PhotoEdit; F43 Mike Yamashita/The Stock Shop; F44 CP Picture Archive (Chuck Stoody); F46 Tom McHugh/Photo Researchers; F49 Erich Lessing/Art Resource, NY; F51 Scala/Art Resource, NY; F52, F53 (t) Lawrence Livermore National Laboratory; F53 (b) Michael Rosenfeld/Tony Stone Images; F54 NASA; F58-F59 Scott Warren; F59 (b) M. Zhilin/M. Newman/Photo Researchers; F60 Jan Butchofsky-Houser/Dave G. Houser; F62 (l) Duomo Photography; F62 (c) William R. Sallaz/Duomo Photography; F62 (r), F63 (bl) Stevn E. Sutton/Duomo Photography; F63 (bc) Duomo Photography; F63 (ti) Ken Gallard Photographics; F63 (t) Gary Bigham/International Stock Photography; F64 © Greg L. Ryan; Sally Beyer/AllStock/PNI; F66 Peter Menzel Photography; F68-F69 Phil Degginger/Bruce Coleman, Inc.; F69 (br) Phil Degginger/Bruce Coleman, Inc.; F69 (t) Ontario Science Centre; F72 (t) Michael J. Schimpf; F74 Tony Stone Images; F76 (l), (c) E.R. Degginger/Bruce Coleman, Inc.; F76 (r) Tony Freeman/PhotoEdit; F78 (t) Tim Beddow/Tony Stone Images; F79 (t) Danila G. Donadoni/Bruce Coleman, Inc.; F80 Norbert Wu/Tony Stone Images; F82 Chuck O'Rear/H. Armstrong Roberts, Inc.; F86-F87 Peter Cade/Tony Stone Images; F88 (l) David Overcash/Bruce Coleman, Inc.; F88 (r) David Young-Wolff/PhotoEdit; F89 (l) Keith Gunnar/Bruce Coleman, Inc.; F89 (r) John Elk, III/Bruce Coleman, Inc.; F90 (t) Dr. Jean M. Bennett; F90 (b) Diane Schiumo/Fundamental Photographs; F94-F95 Jeff Hunter/The Image Bank; F95 (t) Science Photo Library/Photo Researchers; F95 (bl) James King-Holmes/Science Photo Library/Photo Researchers; F95 (br) Ron Chapple/FPG International; F96 Cary Wolinsky/Stock, Boston/PNI; F98 Billy E. Barnes/PhotoEdit; F99 (t) Gary Conner/PhotoEdit; F99 (c) Bill Aron/PhotoEdit; F99 (b) Myrleen Ferguson/PhotoEdit; F100 (br) David Young-Wolfe/PhotoEdit; F100 (tl) Tony Freeman/PhotoEdit/PNI; F102 Jim McCrary/Tony Stone Images; F104 Wendell Metzen/Bruce Coleman, Inc.; F104 (i) Mark E. Gibson; F105 (l) Keith Gunnar/Bruce Coleman, Inc.; F105 (c) Tony Freeman/PhotoEdit; F105 (r) Mark Newman/Bruce Coleman, Inc.; F106 Claus Militz/Okapia/Photo Researchers; F108 Myrleen Ferguson/PhotoEdit; F110 (b) Cameramann International; F110 (t) Alan L. Detrick/Photo Researchers; F111 (b) Glen Allison/Tony Stone Images; F111 (t) Nicholas de Vore III/Bruce Coleman, Inc.; F111 (c) Andrew Rakoczy/Bruce Coleman, Inc.; F112 Lockheed Space and Missile Co., Inc.; F114 Mark E. Gibson; F115 (t) M.E. Rzucidlo/H. Armstrong Roberts, Inc.; F115 (b) Andy Sacks/Tony Stone Images; F116 (t) Drew Donovan Photography; F116 (b) Stan Ries/International Stock Photography; F120 (l) Tony Stone Images; F120 (i) David Zaitz/Photonica

Health Handbook

R20 (c) Tony Freeman/PhotoEdit; R20 (br) David Young-Wolff/PhotoEdit; R21 (t) Myrleen Ferguson Cate/PhotoEdit; R21 (b) David Young-Wolff/PhotoEdit; R23 Tony Freeman/PhotoEdit

All other photographs by Harcourt photographers listed below, © Harcourt: Weronica Ankarorn, Bartlett Digital Photograpy, Victoria Bowen, Eric Camden, Digital Imaging Group, Charles Hodges, Ken Karp, Ken Kinzie, Ed McDonald, Sheri O'Neal, Terry Sinclair